North London
MURDERS

Geoffrey Howse

SUTTON PUBLISHING

First published in the United Kingdom in 2005 by
Sutton Publishing, an imprint of NPI Media Group
Cirencester Road · Chalford · Stroud · Gloucestershire · GL6 8PE

Reprinted 2007

Series Consulting Editor: Stewart P. Evans

British Library Cataloguing in Publication Data
A catalogue record for this book is available from the British Library.

ISBN 978-0-7509-3454-1

This book is dedicated
to the memory of my father
HERBERT HOWSE,
12 May 1916–8 April 2004

Typeset in 10.5/13.5pt Sabon
Typesetting and origination by
Sutton Publishing.
Printed and bound in England.

Contents

Introduction

The boroughs we refer to as North London, including the north-east and north-west of the capital, cover a large area and over the centuries have witnessed literally thousands of murders. Within the pages of this book are some of the cases that have attracted the curiosity of the public and commentators, both at the time and in the years that have followed. Some of them were milestones in the annals of crime detection.

The earliest murder included here is that of Sir Edmund Berry Godfrey, a crime committed during the reign of Charles II which, although unsolved, resulted in the execution of three innocent men. The Steinberg murder and suicide case occurred during the reign of William IV and is particularly unusual — for the aftermath if not for the crime itself — and the Islington 'baby farming' case serves to illustrate the depths of depravity to which certain sectors of Victorian and Edwardian society had sunk. Britain's first railway murder is noteworthy for the way in which the culprit was caught, as is the case of the murder of Henry Smith by Albert Milsom and Henry Fowler at Muswell Hill in 1896. No volume covering the murders of this part of London would be complete without an examination of the Crippen case, but the name of Frederick Henry Seddon, hanged for poisoning Miss Eliza Barrow, is less well known these days, although for several decades following his conviction his waxwork effigy was a popular exhibit in Madame Tussaud's Chamber of Horrors. Seddon was a not very likeable man who may well have been the victim of his own lack of affability, a character trait that went against him at his trial.

The case of the notorious bigamist and wife killer George Joseph Smith is a most unusual one. Although his serial killing took him all around England, he committed his final murder just a short distance from my North London home. In fact, the search for traces of many of the murders included here has been a local one for me. Crippen and Seddon committed their crimes a little over a mile from where I am writing and Ruth Ellis, the last woman to be hanged in Britain, shot her lover David Blakely in 1955 outside the Magdala Tavern, Hampstead, situated just less than two miles away.

In my search for information I have returned to the original documents pertaining to each case in an attempt to give an accurate, comprehensive account. I have gathered evidence from a wide range of sources including contemporary documents, accounts of inquests, newspaper articles and trial transcripts.

Geoffrey Howse
January 2005

1

Death of a Magistrate

THE KILLING OF SIR EDMUND BERRY GODFREY

Primrose Hill, 1678

Sir Edmund Berry Godfrey was the victim of a most puzzling murder, often described as the greatest unsolved crime of the seventeenth century.* His death was surrounded by mystery, intrigue and deceit, and is marked by a false confession that resulted in the execution of three innocent men for a crime they neither committed nor played any part in.

Godfrey's death appears to have come about as a result of his involvement, in his capacity as a magistrate, in the swearing of documents concerning the conspiracy known to history as the 'Popish Plot'. This conspiracy was later proven to be completely false and was in fact the invention of Dr Titus Oates, clergyman, and Dr Israel Tonge, Presbyterian minister and scientist, described by one commentator as a 'fourth-rate parson and a third-rate scientist'. In August 1678 they claimed to have evidence of a Jesuit conspiracy to kill King Charles II and enthrone his brother James, Duke of York, by armed rebellion. The allegations and accusations that followed focused on the currents of anti-Catholicism that had been circulating in the English political system for generations. The revelations made by Oates and Tonge brought all the old fears and prejudices to the forefront. Just as details of the alleged plot were being openly discussed, the killing of the highly regarded Protestant magistrate Sir Edmund Berry Godfrey caused panic on the streets of London.

Godfrey was born into an ancient Kentish family on 23 December 1621. He was the son of Thomas and Sarah Godfrey, the fifth son of his father's second marriage, and was educated at Westminster School and Christ Church, Oxford. He completed his education with a European tour and returned to

---

* This account draws on Alan Marshall, *The Strange Death of Edmund Godfrey* (Sutton, 1999).

The magistrate Sir Edmund Berry Godfrey.
(Author's Collection)

England in 1640, where he entered Gray's Inn at the Inns of Court. He later abandoned his legal studies after a serious infirmity rendered him partially deaf and following this retreated to Kent, where he appears to have stayed recuperating during the seven years of the Civil War. A business opportunity came his way in 1650 and he moved back to London, where he took up the trade of wood-monger and coal merchant, originally at a site near Downgate in the City of London. As a bachelor Godfrey did not need a large household of servants, although he could well have afforded this. He made do with just three.

By the late 1660s he was spending some of his time in local politics, and was nominated as alderman in Farringdon ward in 1664. He purchased several proper-ties, including The Swan Inn at Fulham, leased various other buildings, and engaged in several business ventures with his great friend the Irish healer Valentine Greatrakes. At the same time as his various business enterprises were flourishing he was becoming well known as a justice of the peace.

Though an Anglican, Edmund Godfrey had a reputation for his moderation in enforcing the penal laws (statutes restricting an individual's right to vote, hold office, own land and teach on grounds of his religious faith) upon Nonconformists and Catholics. He had the courage to stay in London throughout the plague and rendered help to its victims, which increased his reputation. Similarly, his reaction following the Great Fire of London in 1666, during which he suffered personal injury while helping others, made him a notable figure at court. He was rewarded for his service with a knighthood and £200 of silver plate, an honour he at first stubbornly refused to accept, claim-ing he sought no reward. The king himself bestowed the honour and the silver plate included a tankard bearing an inscription in Latin that translates as:

A man truly born for his country; when a terrible fire devastated the City, by the providence of God, and his own merit, he was safe and illustrious in the midst of the flames. Afterwards at the express desire of the King (but deservedly so) Edmund Berry Godfrey was created a Knight, in September 1666. For the rest let the public record speak.

Dr Titus Oates (1649–1705) had been sacked from a naval chaplaincy and a parish in Kent. Feeling slighted by the Protestant Church he turned briefly to Catholicism, joined the Jesuits and afterwards claimed to have received a doctorate of divinity from Salamanca University (although this claim, like so many others he made, was bogus). Oates learned sufficient gossip at the Jesuit College of St Omer to be able to tell a convincing tale when he decided to team up with Dr Israel Tonge, who had lectured in biology to the Royal Society and had developed a fanatical fear of Jesuits. The details they put forward of the Popish Plot were outlined in forty-three articles, which Oates later embroidered. These articles included the murder of the king by three separate and entirely different methods, the murder of the entire Privy Council, the wholesale massacre of Protestants, a French invasion of Ireland, and the enthronement of the Duke of York.

Sir Edmund Berry Godfrey's involvement in these high affairs came about after Oates and Tonge began badgering various court officials to discuss the depositions they wished to make concerning the Popish Plot. To bring the plot into the open they needed to have their depositions sworn by a legal authority. They tried to bring their 'evidence' to the attention of Secretary of State, Sir Joseph Williamson, on 5 September 1678, but Williamson was already aware of Tonge's eccentric reputation and declined to see them. They then looked around for someone that they could trust with such an important affair. Eventually they settled on Godfrey.

Tonge went alone to Sir Edmund's house and told him that he wished to have some information sworn. However, he was not prepared to disclose any details at this stage. Sir Edmund was reluctant to become involved without further clarification, but Tonge eventually persuaded him to meet his 'honourable friends' the following day. On 6 September Israel Tonge, Titus Oates and Christopher Kirby (a scientist who assisted the king with his experiments and who Tonge had used to act as a go-between to familiarise the

A 1679 engraving by Robert White of Titus Oates (1649–1705), the main informer in the Popish Plot. *(Author's collection)*

king with the forty-three articles) visited Sir Edmund at his home. The interview did not go to plan. Godfrey was not impressed with the trio. They tried flattery, which did not achieve the desired effect. Then Tonge told Godfrey that the matter was one of treason and that the king himself already had a copy of the depositions. Godfrey began to think again. The three men before him were at the very least a peculiar-looking lot, but perhaps they might have some genuine information after all.

After the three had departed, events began to escalate. Their efforts to bring the accusations to the authorities were now causing considerable interest and tongues were wagging. On 27 September a summons came from the Privy Council. Tonge and Kirby arrived too late to attend and were told to return the next day, but the informers had now achieved their aim: their accusations would be made before the highest in the land. However, fearful that Oates might be made to disappear from the scene at the hand of the Jesuits, they felt it was essential that the documents should be legally sworn. Once again the three men went to the house of Sir Edmund Berry Godfrey, and there on 27 September Oates swore before the magistrate and Sir Edmund signed two copies of his information, which was witnessed by Tonge and Kirby. Much to their consternation, Sir Edmund insisted that he keep one copy for himself. They reluctantly agreed and left.

Following the swearing of the documents Godfrey was known to have expressed fears to his associates about an attack on his own person. On 12 October a visitor called at Sir Edmund's house in the early morning, sometime before 7 a.m., and was told by a servant he had already gone out. Later that morning Godfrey returned home and a servant, Henry Moor, helped his master dress in his new coat. Sir Edmund then changed his mind and put on a different coat and his sword. He walked to the fields in the north and asked the whereabouts of Paddington Woods, perhaps not such an odd question for a woodmonger. Godfrey was not seen for certain again, although Thomas Grundy and James Huysman claimed that between 2 and 3 p.m. they had seen a man resembling Sir Edmund near the White House at Primrose Hill. Another witness claimed he had seen him after 2 p.m. walking in the fields there, something he had seen Godfrey do often. Various other witnesses came forward with supposed sightings, placing Sir Edmund's movements on that day in the Strand and Lincoln's Inn.

The alarm was raised by Henry Moor. A little after 6 p.m. on the evening of Thursday 17 October 1678, John Brown, Constable of the Parish of Marylebone, led a group of fourteen men to a drainage ditch on a slope at the southern edge of Primrose Hill, close to where the Regent's Canal now runs. At that time the hill was surrounded by open countryside and was a popular beauty spot. A man's body had been reported lying among the brambles there, impaled on a sword. The exact position of the corpse was described as two fields distant from Lower Chalcot Farmhouse. (Lower and Upper Chalcot (or Chalcote, or Chalcott) Farms were on the Chalcot Estate, now commemorated in the area of London known as Chalk Farm.) The body lay in a ditch on one of the slopes of Primrose Hill. It was then known as Greenberry Hill and is now called Barrow Hill. Today the site is marked by a covered reservoir.

Light was fading fast as the group of men approached Greenberry Hill. When they reached the drainage ditch they saw the body of a man lying face down and run through with a sword which had pierced his body from chest to back, and his coat had been thrown over his head. The hilt of the sword was beneath the body and the blade pointed upwards towards the now darkening sky. Constable Brown and another man, William Lock, went into the ditch and turned the body over. They pulled back the victim's coat which covered his face but did not immediately recognise the corpse as being that of Sir Edmund Berry Godfrey, although both men were aware of Godfrey's disappearance five days previously. The constable removed the sword from the body, which was then carried over several fields to a nearby inn, the White House. Other items left near the body were also taken there, including a hat, scabbard, belt, stick and gloves. All belonged to the deceased.

When the group of men arrived at the White House, the corpse was identified as the missing magistrate. On examination it was discovered that before the victim had been run through with his own sword, he had been strangled and beaten about the body from head to stomach, and other stab wounds had been inflicted after death.

On Friday 18 October a coroner's jury was assembled at the White House by the Coroner of Middlesex, John Cooper. Before proceedings began Mr White, Coroner of Westminster, arrived, apparently at the request of the residents of Godfrey's home parish of St Martin's in the Fields, who wanted their own man to oversee the proceedings. Mr White offered to assist Mr Cooper or even to take charge of events. Both offers were refused. An altercation took place which made both men look foolish and was finally settled when Mr White went away, having being given a guinea for his troubles by Sir Edmund's brother Michael. Proceedings got under way and as the debate reached the point where the verdict swayed between one of suicide or murder, the coroner decided to adjourn until the following morning. Because of the general disruption caused by the large crowd that had gathered at the White House, the coroner decided to change the venue to The Rose and Crown in St Giles. The inquest resumed there the following morning and the jury was still in attendance at midnight, presumably because of the large number of witnesses called. The verdict was wilful murder by persons unknown and that he had been strangled.

Exactly who killed Sir Edmund Berry Godfrey will probably never be known. If, as the evidence appears to suggest, his death was a direct result of

Charles II. *(Author's Collection)*

the part he played in bringing to notice the Popish Plot, then one might assume that the Jesuits played some part in the crime. However, as the plot was later shown to be complete fabrication, then that possibility seems unlikely. Perhaps Godfrey's death was engineered by the creators of the plot to add credence to their claims.

In December 1678, several weeks after the discovery of Godfrey's body, a Catholic silversmith, Miles Prance, who was at that time being detained for conspiracy, confessed under torture to complicity in Godfrey's murder. His evidence was corroborated by the informer William Bedloe. Prance's story was that as Godfrey passed Somerset House on his way from St Clement Dane's, he was lured to a spot near the Watergate and there he was strangled. The body was then concealed in various parts of Somerset House for several days. It was later carried in a sedan chair to Covent Garden, where it was transferred to a horse and taken to Primrose Hill. There it was impaled on the sword and flung in a ditch. Three men were named as being involved in the plot – Robert Green, Henry Berry and Lawrence Hill. They were arrested. There were apparently others, including two Catholic priests, who escaped. Green, Berry and Hill were convicted on the flimsiest circumstantial evidence and executed in 1679, but Prance's 'confession' was afterwards declared false and he pleaded guilty to perjury. Was it simply coincidence that the surnames of the three men spelled out the exact spot where Sir Edmund's body was found, Greenberry Hill? It is with good reason that this case has been referred to as the greatest unsolved crime of the seventeenth century.

In the East Cloister at Westminster Abbey there is a memorial to Sir Edmund, placed there by his brother Benjamin in 1696 with the Godfrey family memorial. The inscription is in Latin. The English translation reads:

Edmund Berry Godfrey made knight on account of his loyal service to the king and country. He discharged the office of magistrate with notable trustworthiness and diligence, was finally snatched from the eyes of his

The Godfrey memorial in Westminster Abbey. *(Alan Marshall)*

family four days before the ides of October 1678. Five days later he was discovered murdered in a shocking and criminal manner and of the other details let History speak. His monument was repaired having been eroded by time, with an addition of a eulogy of his brother Edmund, by Benjamin, the youngest son of Thomas Godfrey and the rest of his line, 4 April 1696.

As for the instigators of the Popish Plot, the meeting of the Privy Council at which Oates and Tonge were to be questioned took place on 28 and 29 September, and the whole can of worms was then opened. Oates's ridiculous accusations would no doubt have been exposed when he was examined by the Privy Council had it not been discovered that Edward Coleman, the Duchess of York's secretary, had been engaged in treasonable correspondence with the Jesuit La Chaise, Louis XIV's reputed *éminence grise*. Coleman's letters were more foolish than treacherous, but they were enough to send him to the scaffold. Oates enjoyed a temporary spot in the limelight and during this time he even accused Queen Caroline of plotting to poison the king. Following Oates's accusations a series of state trials of Catholics took place, starting with that of Coleman with Oates as principal witness for the prosecution. As a result Edward Coleman was executed in December 1678, the first of at least thirty-five men to be judicially murdered.

Tonge died before he could be brought to justice for his part in the affair. Oates was tried and convicted of perjury after the Duke of York came to the throne as James II in 1685. The notorious Judge Jeffreys imposed a severe sentence on Oates. He was deprived of his clerical habit, given a heavy fine, had to make five appearances in the pillory annually, was subjected to a whipping from Aldgate to Newgate on 20 May 1685 and a whipping from Newgate to Tyburn on 22 May; then he was to be imprisoned for life. Despite the whippings, which were carried out mercilessly, Oates survived and spent the remainder of James's reign in Newgate. He was released after James's downfall and the accession of William III and Mary II. He married a well-off widow in 1693, was given £500 by the government in 1698 to pay his debts, became a Baptist preacher at Wapping Chapel, and was expelled from the Baptist movement in 1701 as a 'disorderly person and a hypocrite'. He died in 1705.

2

Murder of Innocents

Clerkenwell, 1834 and Islington, 1902–3

THE KILLING OF ELLEN LEFEVRE AND HER FOUR CHILDREN

In the yard of the parish church of St James, Clerkenwell, stands a gravestone that marks the resting place of the victims of one of the most brutal murders committed during the reign of King William IV. Its motive, if indeed there was one, has never been explained. On the gravestone, now considerably weathered, part of the inscription is just discernible. The stone was erected by public subscription and marks the spot where Ellen Lefevre, aged 25, and her four children, aged between 6 years and 8 months, were buried after they were slain by their father, Ellen's long-time lover, on the night of 8 September 1834.

Ellen Lefevre and her children were all killed by having their throats cut from ear to ear. The evidence suggested that this was not just a savage act carried out by a deranged father while his defenceless prey slept, as two of the victims had been much mutilated in their struggles for life. Johan (John) Nicholas Steinberg, a German, was a 45-year-old whipmaker. He lived with Ellen Lefevre, a lady later described as his mistress, and their four children at 17 Southampton Street, now renamed Calshot Street, a turning off the Pentonville Road. The present-day Calshot Street bears little resemblance to the Southampton Street that existed in the early nineteenth century. Street numbering has twice undergone a change since that period and few old buildings remain in what has become a semi-industrial thoroughfare. Why Steinberg murdered Ellen and their children will never be known, because having perpetrated this brutal act he fell upon the knife, without leaving any explanation or clue as to his motives.

Discovery of this crime was not immediate. However, once it was realised that something was amiss at the Steinberg household a forced entry was effected. It was then that the shocking discovery was made. Those in attendance at the murder scene described it as one of the most dreadful they

The parish church of St James,
Clerkenwell. Ellen Lefevre and her four
children are buried in the churchyard.
(Paul T. Langley Welch)

had ever witnessed. Every room had the appearance of a slaughterhouse and was deluged with blood. John Steinberg's blood-soaked body was found in the back kitchen. The white-handled knife with which he had committed the crime lay beneath him.

On 11 September the bodies were removed from the murder scene in shells. When the shell containing Steinberg was brought out of the house, the large crowd that had gathered in Southampton Street shouted abuse, and suggested that his body should be kicked through the streets. An inquest was held at The Three Kings in Clerkenwell Close. Afterwards the funeral of the murder victims was held at public expense. They were given a decent burial and a gravestone was erected, thanks to the generosity of local people and outraged strangers. The inscription reads:

A wonderful and horrible thing is committed in the land.
– Jer. Ch.5, v.30.

Beneath this stone are deposited the remains of Ellen Lefevre, aged 25 years, and her four children.

Henry aged 5 years and 6 months
John aged 4 years and 6 months
Ellen aged 2 years and 6 months
Philip aged 8 months

Who were murdered at their residence in Southampton-street, Pentonville, during the night of 8th of September, 1834, by John Nicholas Steinberg, aged 45 years, a native of Germany, and father of the above children, who afterwards murdered himself, and was buried according to law.

> Poor babes could not your innocence prevail!
> And when your father heard your plaintive wail
> Did no compunction smite his guilty soul,
> Dark thoughts of murder to control
> None!
> None heard your cries, in sleep the world was bound,
> A gloomy, death-like stillness reigned around,
> While guilt with gliding footsteps noiseless trod,
> You slept on earth, you woke and saw your God.
> 'Neath your creator's wings in peace you're blest,
> For angels wafted you to realms of rest.

This stone was erected by public subscription to commemorate the lamentable event.

> Where is the flock that was given thee, thy beautiful flock?
> – Jer. Ch.13, v.20

> His remembrance shall perish from the earth, and he shall have no name in the street. – Job Ch.18, v.17

The epitaph was composed by Mr Campbell, formerly of Sadler's Wells.

Steinberg himself was given an entirely different type of burial in the Pauper's Burial Ground in Ray Street, Clerkenwell. As with many such graveyards, the site of this burial ground was redeveloped during the 1850s, just a few years after Steinberg had committed his crime. William Pinks in his *History of Clerkenwell*, written over twenty years after the murders, describes Steinberg's funeral:

At this ignominious funeral, which took place at night, a peculiar ceremony in lieu of the old custom of driving a stake through the body was observed. The shell containing the deceased was laid by the side of the grave; the body was taken out by two men who held it over the grave; when they gave it a turn it fell to the bottom with the face downwards resting upon the arms. Some earth was scattered over and then one of the assistants struck the earth immediately over the deceased's skull several times, and as hard as he could with an iron mallet, the object being to break the skull.

This burial of a murderer and suicide attracted a considerable number of spectators, and one quick-thinking entrepreneur realised that the general public's morbid curiosity could lead to a healthy profit. William Pinks states that one newspaper report on 29 September 1834 read:

The Steinberg murder — The house in Southampton Street, Pentonville, was on Monday last taken possession of by the new tenant, to whom it has been let by Mr Cuthbert, the landlord, at the yearly rent of £28, being £2 less than the amount paid by Steinberg himself, and yesterday the premises were submitted to the inspection of the public, each person paying a trifle according to his circumstances. The house remains in exactly the same state as it was when viewed by the Coroner's Jury, with the exception that some part of the flooring has been attempted to be cleaned; but the blood was found to have saturated so deeply into the wood, that the stains could not be effaced without planing a great part of it away. The whole of the premises have at present a most melancholy and desolate appearance. It appears that the house has been taken by the present occupant, joined with two or three other persons, on the speculation solely of showing it to the public; and, to render the sight as attractive as possible to lovers of the horrific, this scene of cruel butchery is intended to display a set of wax composition figures, vividly representing the murderer and his victims, and wearing the identical clothing they had on at the time the murder was perpetrated. It is stated that the enormous sum of £25 was given for the clothes in question. The figures were expected yesterday afternoon, and for hours Southampton-street was thronged by persons who anxiously waited taking their chance of catching a sight of them as they were being carried in. The speculation promises to turn out a profitable one, as in the course of yesterday nearly £50 was taken. The adjoining houses either side have become vacant. Two police constables were in attendance to preserve order.

This macabre and distasteful exhibition aroused mixed feelings in the area. Mr Rogers, the local magistrate, received numerous complaints from residents regarding the gross nuisance that occurred in Southampton Street following the opening of No. 17 to the paying public. Formal complaints were also made to various parish officers and the exhibition was finally closed down, but not before a substantial profit had been made by those anxious to benefit from the tragedy of others.

THE ISLINGTON BABY-FARMING CASE

Baby-farming was a peculiarity of late Victorian England: unwanted babies and children, whether illegitimate or simply a burden to their parents, were farmed out to women who acted as foster-mothers. These women were paid to 'adopt' the children or to look after them for a specified period, before they were moved to permanent homes. Large financial rewards could be obtained by taking these unwanted children and the result was that some women obtained money to place a child in a good home and, having found none, 'took care' of their charges simply by killing them. Two such women were Amelia Sach and Annie Walters.

A golden opportunity hiding behind the doors of an outwardly respectable establishment offered itself to this unscrupulous couple. The number of private nursing homes was increasing during the late Victorian age and this type of enterprise, suitably managed, could work hand in glove with baby-farming. One such nursing home advertised its services in North London and was owned by the younger of the two killers, Mrs Amelia Sach, aged 26. She lived at Claymore House in Hertford Road, East Finchley, which she had converted to serve as a private lying-in hospital. There she operated a successful business as an *accoucheuse*. She claimed to be a certified midwife and nurse and attended to her female patients herself. In difficult cases she arranged for a doctor to be present.

Her accomplice was 51-year-old Annie Walters, a married lady who described herself as a 'short-stay foster parent'. It will never be known exactly how many unfortunate babies lost their lives as a result of coming into contact with these women. Sach and Walters certainly had the opportunity and the financial incentive to make use of their position of trust in whatever way best suited their own interests. Everything seemed to be going well with their enterprise until Mrs Walters decided to change address. She was fond of moving and appears to have done so frequently, but this final change of address brought about her downfall and also that of her accomplice. At the time of her arrest on 18 November 1902 Walters was living at 11 Danbury Street, Islington; she had been there since 29 October. Her short stay in Danbury Street was to make No. 11 one of the most notorious addresses in North London, such was the outrage the case caused.

Mrs Walters's landlord in Danbury Street lived on the premises with his wife. As well as taking in lodgers, Mr Sale was a police constable. His wife was beguiled by Mrs Walters's caring manner and was deceived by her tales of being an experienced foster-mother who looked after unfortunate children until suitable adoptive parents could be found – often wealthy, well-to-do couples who whisked the babies away to lives of luxury and opportunity. However, Mrs Walters's fanciful stories did not ring true with Police Constable Sale. Her many accounts of how babies were given new homes made him suspicious. He discussed the matter with a colleague, Detective Constable George Wright, and they decided that the number of adoptions, conducted sometimes in the street if Mrs Walters was to be believed, seemed unlikely.

No. 11 Danbury Street, Islington, which featured in the baby-farming case of 1902–3. *(Paul T. Langley Welch)*

Then events took a new turn. Mrs Walters drew attention to her activities when she asked a fellow lodger at 11 Danbury Street, Mrs Spencer, to do some shopping for her. She gave Mrs Spencer a £1 note with which to buy some carbolic acid and a bottle of chlorodyne. When Police Constable Sale heard about these purchases, his curiosity was aroused. What could his lodger possibly want with such items? The first had disinfectant properties, often used to disguise the smell of something unpleasant; the other was a patent narcotic and anodyne. He and his colleague came to the conclusion that further investigation was warranted and they decided to watch Mrs Walters closely.

On 18 November Annie Walters had in her possession a baby boy, believed to be the child of Ada Galley, a single young woman and a patient at Claymore House, East Finchley, who had given birth a few days previously. Detective Constable Wright observed Walters leaving Danbury Street with the baby and followed her to South Kensington railway station. After watching her movements for some time, he demanded to see the child. The baby boy was dead. Wright took Walters into custody at King's Cross police station. Dr Caunter, acting divisional surgeon, examined the body of the infant and concluded that it had been dead for between 8 and 12 hours. When she was arrested Mrs Walters told the police, 'I never murdered the dear. I only gave it two drops in its bottle, the same as I take myself.' After a little further investigation Mrs Walter's statement soon put Mrs Sach in the frame. Many witnesses came forward and a strong case against them was quickly formed.

Following an inquest, on Friday 2 January 1903 the *Islington Daily Gazette and North London Tribune* reported:

The Deputy-Coroner, in summing up, said the jury had to say whether they were satisfied that the deceased came from the house of Mrs Sach; secondly, whether it was handed over to Mrs Walters when it was alive; and thirdly, whether its death arose from the wilful neglect of Mrs Walters, and also against Mrs Sach. If they found that so, then they must find a verdict of wilful murder against Mrs Walters, and also against Mrs Sach as an accessory before the fact. Mrs Walters and Mrs Sach had had an opportunity of coming there and giving evidence explaining their position; but they had not accepted the opportunity. He had no power to force them to attend, and he would strongly urge the jury not to attach too much importance to their refusal to attend, as they might be acting on the advice of their legal representatives.

The jury returned after an absence of five minutes, and in reply to the usual question, the foreman said they found a verdict of 'Wilful murder' against Mrs Walters, and found that Mrs Sach was an accessory before the fact.

The witnesses were afterwards bound over to attend the trial at the Central Criminal Court.

The date of the trial was set for 15 January. It was presided over by Mr Justice Darling. As the trial proceeded and the catalogue of events unfolded, the public were reminded of the Dyer case, which had taken place in May 1896. Mrs Amelia Elizabeth Dyer, a 57-year-old murderess known as the 'Reading baby-farmer' had killed at least seven children. Her motive had been greed: she charged boarding fees for infants placed in her care, although the infants themselves were quickly disposed of. Her defence's plea of insanity was disregarded and she was executed at Newgate on 10 June 1896.

The trial revealed how the two women worked but it also served another purpose: many newspaper reports helped to highlight the fact that these two women were not the only ones engaged in this activity. It was Annie Walters's stupidity that brought an end to this pair's activities, but their crime has been described as a national phenomenon, a social problem arising from the restrictive nature of Victorian society. Unwanted babies and children were being disposed of all over the country, a fact that the authorities of the time steadfastly refused to recognise. The case served to highlight the plight of single women who found themselves pregnant and unable to take on the responsibility of bringing up a child themselves. In some cases, if they kept the child, both mother and infant would suffer great hardship. Women such as Sach and Walters were quick to capitalise on the misfortunes of these vulnerable mothers. For a fee of £25 or £30 (about £1,500–£1,800 at today's values) Mrs Sach offered to place the infants with good families and the children usually left Claymore House, East Finchley, in the care of Mrs Annie Walters.

On 12 November 1902 an unmarried woman, Miss Pardoe, the lady-friend of a sanitary engineer, was a patient at Claymore House. She earned her own living and was keen to have her child adopted. Mrs Sach assured her she had five wealthy ladies eager to take the baby. Papers were signed which later proved that Miss Pardoe had given Mrs Sach two £10 notes and two £5 notes. The child, a girl, was duly delivered by Mrs Sach herself on 13 November, and later that same day a telegram was sent to Mrs Walters in Danbury Street. It read: 'Five o'clock tonight, Sach Finchley.'

Mrs Walters left Danbury Street that afternoon and returned in the evening carrying a bundle. It was then that she gave Mrs Spencer the £1 note with which to purchase the carbolic acid and chlorodyne. Walters was seen with the baby at 11 Danbury Street the next day and on the morning that followed she was seen leaving her lodgings carrying a bundle. Witnesses next reported seeing her at 3 o'clock in a Lockhart's Cocoa Room in Whitechapel, an area she often frequented. The evidence of a witness who saw Walters in this establishment and others who testified to her carrying a bundle that afternoon proved damning. One of the assistants at Lockhart's, Miss Ethel Jones, remembered the bundle. When part of the wrap fell away, she noticed a doll-like creature, which showed no signs of movement. Other witnesses testified that they had seen Mrs Walters carrying 'doll-like bundles' in various places on numerous occasions. The baby seen that Friday afternoon in Lockhart's was never seen again. Mrs Walters may have left the dead child on a rubbish tip, which was not at all uncommon during that period, or on waste ground, or as has often been speculated – as Mrs Walters was fond of living near the canal – perhaps she simply threw her bundle in the water.

Regarding the dead baby boy, Mrs Walters's actions were discovered on 18 November. When Dr Caunter examined the child he discovered that the boy's clothes smelled of carbolic acid. As for the pitiful little body, 'the jaws were clenched, toes turned inward, hands tightly clenched'. He considered the organs to be normal. However, he concluded that the child died of asphyxia. Chlorodyne, a painkiller containing morphia, chloroform and prussic acid, mixed with a baby's milk in sufficient quantity would soon cause death; and carbolic acid was presumably used as a disinfectant, to disguise the offensive odours of a body in the early stages of decomposition. If the dead baby had been disposed of in some public place, among the refuse, the use of carbolic acid would have given sufficient short-term protection against detection until the remains were removed with the refuse to a place where their discovery would be unlikely. When the evidence gathered for the coroner's court was combined with the evidence gathered for the trial itself, the case against Sach and Walters was overwhelming. The outcome of the trial was almost a foregone conclusion.

On Monday 19 January 1903 the *Islington Daily Gazette and North London Tribune* ran an article almost lost among its advertisements for attractions at local theatres (at the newly decorated Islington Empire the Boisnet Troupe was headlining that week, and at the Holloway Empire Happy Fanny Fields and the Collins Trio were the main attractions). The newspaper reported the trial under the heading 'CONDEMNED TO DEATH':

An engraving of Holloway Prison as it looked from 1849 to 1970. *(Author's collection)*

What has been called the Islington child murder case has come to an end, with the condemnation to death of the two heartless women who, for paltry sums of money, put to death infant children born at a midwifery establishment of the kind that trades on the misfortunes of unmarried women. There could be no other verdict or sentence. The sanctity of human life must be upheld by the law. It is notoriously outraged by women who as mothers or as baby-farmers annually abandon hundreds of newly born children in the streets or elsewhere, but very seldom come within the grasp of the law. Mrs Dyer was a dreadful type of this class of callous murderer, and it cannot be said there is much difference between the offences of that monster and the women Sach and Walters, who now await their doom. In both cases there was the same unwomanly callousness, the same spirit of savagery, and although an illogical jury found some reason for mercy on the ground that they were 'women', we question if their right to the title will be admitted. Exceptional murder from the excitement of passion may sometimes claim a merciful consideration, but systematic, cold-blooded, wholesome murder is past human concession.

Mrs Sach's plea for clemency on the grounds that it was most unusual to be hanged as an accessory was turned down and the two women were executed at Holloway Prison by the Billington brothers on 3 February 1903. It was the first double female execution in Britain for some years and the first ever at Holloway.

3

Britain's First Railway Murder

FRANZ MÜLLER AND THE MURDER
OF THOMAS BRIGGS

Hackney Wick, 1864

On Saturday 9 July 1864 Thomas Briggs, chief clerk at Messrs Robarts & Co. of Lombard Street, left the bank in the afternoon as was his usual custom. During the evening he dined with his niece and her husband, Mr and Mrs David Buchan, at 23 Nelson Square, Peckham (today's Furley Road), before he returned to the city to catch a suburban train on the North London Railway, which left Fenchurch Street station for Chalk Farm at 9.50 p.m. He travelled in a first-class carriage, Carriage No. 69. Mr Briggs lived at 5 Clapton Square, near to the Hackney or Hackney Wick (Victoria Park) stations, in north-east London.

The train left the next station, Bow, at 10.01 p.m., Hackney Wick at 10.05 p.m. and arrived at Hackney at approximately 10.11 p.m. At this station two bank clerks who were also employed by Messrs Robarts & Co., Henry Vernez and Sydney Jones, who had purchased tickets for Highbury, opened the door of a first-class compartment, which was unoccupied, got in and sat down. Almost immediately Sydney Jones felt something wet and drew his companion's attention to some blood on his hand. They immediately left the carriage and summoned the guard of the train, Benjamin Ames. Mr Ames examined the compartment and discovered bloodstains on the cushions of the seat that backed onto the engine on the left-hand side of the train as it was going from London. There was blood on the glass by the cushion, some blood on the cushion opposite and on the offside handle of the carriage door. In the carriage the guard found a hat, a walking stick and a small black leather bag. He took these away and the carriage was locked. The train continued on its

Thomas Briggs. *(Stewart P. Evans)*

journey to Chalk Farm and was later taken back to Bow. Mr Greenwood, the stationmaster at Chalk Farm, took charge of the hat, walking stick and bag as lost property.

The driver and guard of a train travelling through north-east London at about the same time as the hat, walking stick and bag were being handed to Mr Greenwood at Chalk Farm made an alarming discovery. They were taking a train of empty carriages from Hackney Wick station to Fenchurch Street and had just crossed the railway bridge by Victoria Park when William Timms, the guard, was alerted by Alfred Ekin, the engine-driver, to something lying in the 6ft way between the Up and Down lines. They stopped the train and backed it up to where the object was lying. When they went to investigate they discovered the body of a man lying on his back with his head towards Hackney. Help was summoned from the nearby Mitford Castle pub and the body was carried along a path down the embankment at the side of the railway bridge and into the inn.

Police Constable K71, Edward Dougan, was quickly on the scene. Having detected signs of life he immediately sent for a surgeon, Vincent Merton Cooper. Before medical help arrived PC Dougan searched the victim's pockets. In the left-hand trouser pocket he found four sovereigns and some keys; in the vest pocket a florin and half a first-class railway ticket; in the right-hand trouser pocket 10s 6d in silver and copper, some more keys, a silver snuffbox, various letters and papers and a silk handkerchief. The man also wore a diamond ring on the little finger of his right hand and there was a gold fastening to his waistcoat. His identity was established by a bundle of letters in his pocket, which bore his full address: 'T. Briggs, Esq., Robarts & Co., Lombard Street'. Mr Briggs had several severe wounds, apparently inflicted by a blunt instrument used to ferocious effect, and other injuries, bruises and contusions, which those who attended him following the attack suggested might have been sustained when he fell from the carriage. Mr Briggs's own surgeon, Francis Toulmin of Lower Clapton, arrived at the Mitford Castle a little before 3 a.m. He found Mr Briggs groaning but unconscious; Briggs died

The discovery of the body of Thomas Briggs. *(Stewart P. Evans)*

at 11.45 p.m. on Sunday night, approximately 27 hours after the attack had taken place.

A post-mortem examination was carried out on the body on Tuesday 12 July by Mr Toulmin attended by Mr Brereton, Mr Cooper and others. He described the condition of Mr Briggs, who stood about 5ft 9in tall and weighed between 11 and 12 stones. After describing the severe head injuries, Mr Toulmin concluded that the superficial injuries sustained by Mr Briggs to the left side of his head were consistent with his fall from the railway carriage and the other injuries to his head were consistent with his having been struck by a blunt instrument four or five times.

Mr Briggs's friends were contacted and it was established that when he left home on the morning of the murderous attack, he wore gold-rimmed glasses and a gold watch and chain. The stick and bag were his, but not the hat. A desperate struggle must have taken place in the carriage, and the stains of a bloody hand marked the door. The facts of the murder and its object, robbery, were thus conclusively proved. It was also easily established that the hat found in the carriage had been bought at Walker's, a hatter's in Crawford Street, Marylebone, while within a few days Mr Briggs's gold chain was traced to a jeweller's at 55 Cheapside. The jeweller, Mr Death, had given another in exchange for it to a man thought to be a foreigner. More precise clues to the murderer's identity were not long wanting; indeed the readiness with which they were produced and followed up showed how the wide dissemination of news regarding a murder facilitates the detection of crime. In a little more than a week a cabman came forward and voluntarily made a statement which at once drew suspicion to a German, Franz Müller, who had been the man's lodger. Müller had given the cabman's little daughter a jeweller's cardboard box bearing the name of Mr Death. A photograph of Müller shown to the jeweller was identified as the likeness of the man who had exchanged Mr Briggs's chain. Last of all, the cabman swore that he had bought the very hat found in the carriage for Müller at Walker's of Crawford Street, Marylebone.

This fixed the crime squarely on Müller, who had already left the country, thus increasing the suspicion under which he lay. There was no mystery about his departure: he had gone to Canada by the *Victoria* sailing ship, starting from London docks and bound for New York. When these facts were established two detectives armed with an arrest warrant, and

Franz Müller. *(Author's collection)*

accompanied by the jeweller and the cabman, went to Liverpool and took the first steamer across the Atlantic. This was the *City of Manchester*, and it was expected to arrive some days before the *Victoria*. When the sailing ship docked, the officers boarded the *Victoria* at once, Müller was identified by Mr Death, and the arrest was made. Mr Briggs's watch was found wrapped up in a piece of leather in the suspect's luggage, and at the time of his capture Müller was actually wearing Mr Briggs's hat, cut down and somewhat altered. The prisoner was extradited to England immediately. He and his escort arrived on 17 September.

Franz Müller, aged 25, was a native of Saxe-Weimar. In his native country he had been apprenticed as a gunsmith and had arrived in England in 1862 hoping to find work. Unable to secure a job in his chosen trade, he found work as a tailor and was last employed in that capacity for a six-week period up to 2 July 1864 by Mr Hodgkinson of Threadneedle Street, at 25s a week. At the time of the murder Müller was lodging at 16 Park Terrace, which was part of the Old Ford Road, Victoria Park, Hackney.

His trial followed at the next sessions of the Central Criminal Court and began on 27 October 1864. It lasted for three days and ended in his conviction. The case was one of circumstantial evidence, but, as Sir Robert Collyer, the Solicitor-General, pointed out, it was the strongest circumstantial evidence ever been brought forward in a murder case and it could not be explained away. Collyer cited the prisoner's poverty, his inability to account for himself on the night of the murder, and his possession of the property of the murdered man. An alibi was set up for the defence but not well substantiated, and without hesitation the jury returned a verdict of guilty.

Müller protested after sentence of death had been passed upon him that he had been convicted on a false statement of facts. He adhered to this almost to the very last. His case had been warmly espoused by the Society for the Protection of Germans in the United Kingdom, and powerful influence was exerted both in England and abroad to obtain a reprieve. Müller knew that any confession would ruin his chances of escape. His arguments were specious and evasive when pressed to confess. 'Why should man confess to man?' he replied. 'Man cannot forgive man, only God can do so. Man is therefore only accountable to God.' But on the gallows, when the cap was over his eyes and the rope had been adjusted round his neck, he whispered into the ear of the German pastor who attended him on the scaffold: 'I did it.' Dr Cappel passed on Müller's words to the assembled members of the press in the Chaplain's Room immediately after the execution.

However, Dr Cappel was perhaps a little overzealous in his enthusiasm after he left the scaffold. His comments resulted in long-lasting controversy concerning the exact wording of Müller's supposed confession. A letter to the editor of the *Sporting Times* on 19 March 1887 read:

Lord Chief Baron (Sir Frederick) Pollock, presiding judge at the trial of Franz Müller. *(Author's collection)*

Mr Hardinge Gifford, one of the counsel for the Crown. *(Author's collection)*

Sir R.P. Collyer QC, MP (first Lord Monkswell), who led the counsel for the Crown. *(Author's collection)*

Mr Serjeant Parry, who led the counsel for the defence. *(Author's collection)*

Dear Corlett, – In your account last week of the trial and execution of Franz Müller, whose defence, you may remember, was entrusted to my care, you state that Müller's last words, in reply to Dr Cappel's question, were, 'Yes I have done it.' This is incorrect. What he said was, 'Ich habe.' He had no time to finish the sentence, which might have been 'Ich habe es nicht getan' (I have not done it). His innocence or guilt, therefore, so far as his own confession is concerned, must ever remain a moot point.

Your giving publicity to this will oblige,

yours faithfully, THO. BEARD, 10 Basinghall Street.

There was a great deal of correspondence relating to Müller's last words in subsequent issues of the *Sporting Times*. Accounts vary considerably in content, but whether or not Müller actually confessed is of little consequence, as the evidence against him was incontrovertible. While in the condemned cell Müller conversed freely with the warders in broken English or through an interpreter. In official descriptions Müller was described as 'not bad-looking', with a 'square, German type of face', blue eyes (which were generally half closed) and very fair hair. He was short in stature and his legs were light for the upper part of his body, which was powerful, almost herculean.

It is generally supposed that Franz Müller's motives for murdering Thomas Briggs were covetousness and greed. He saw Mr Briggs's watch-chain, and followed him instantly into the carriage, determined to have it at all costs. Mr Briggs was carrying a not inconsiderable sum of his own cash at the time of the attack, and this money and other valuables remained untouched, which seems to indicate that the attack was swift and that the assailant panicked and left the scene of his crime quickly. Mr Briggs might have been dozing and Müller, in his attempt to steal the watch and chain, may have woken him up and met with resistance. The evidence left at the scene of the crime and the general opinion of the time was that Müller attacked Mr Briggs with the victim's own walking stick. Having realised the enormity of his actions, Müller clearly panicked. He either dragged his victim to the carriage door and pushed him out, or Mr Briggs might somehow have been attempting to flee from his assailant's blows and in a semi-conscious state opened the carriage door and fell mortally injured onto the 6ft way. Certainly a violent and bloody attack took place. Whatever happened inside first-class carriage No. 69, Müller fled the scene at the earliest opportunity, and in doing so clumsily left an important clue that led to his early detection and subsequent conviction for wilful murder.

Müller received his death sentence on 29 October 1864. This was the first British train murder and as such received a great deal of media attention, both immediately following Mr Briggs's death and after Müller's arrest and trial. In fact this case caused considerable unease among railway passengers, because it highlighted the dangers of travelling in badly lit railway compartments with no means of intercommunication. It is hardly surprising that the actual execution attracted a large crowd numbering many thousands. (Public executions were not outlawed until 1868.)

Frederick Wicks, a sub-editor of the *Globe*, was actually present on the scaffold and left an interesting account of the case, some of which is reproduced here.

We met the Sheriffs in the London Coffee-house, on Ludgate Hill, at seven o'clock, and shortly afterwards went round by way of Paternoster Row to a hole that had been made in the wall, through which we passed into the Court-house of the Old Bailey. After a short halt we passed into the chapel yard of the prison, and there we came in view of Müller, standing beside his gaoler, uncovered and apparently unconcerned, waiting for us. The grey light of the chill November morning gave the pair a weird look as they stood on the other side of an open doorway, for it was impossible to divest the scene of the knowledge of what was about to happen.

As we approached, the gaoler led the way with Müller through other courts, and then through a corridor with black stone walls on each side, stone pavement underfoot, and an iron grating overhead, between us and the sky. I have often wondered since whether Müller knew that this corridor was the burial place of those who were hanged, and the place where he would be buried a few hours afterwards, buried in quicklime under those heavy paving stones, with no record but his initials rudely carved on the stone wall, and that only because he was a more than ordinarily famous murderer.

From this grim sepulchre we passed to the Press room, a small chamber, low in the ceiling, and very much like a kitchen, with a deal table and some wooden chairs in it. Here we met Calcraft [the hangman], and the duties of the gaoler were at an end. I had never seen Calcraft before, and I was very much struck with his benevolent and even amiable appearance. His snowy-white hair and beard, and his quiet, self-possessed manner, was in ridiculous contrast to everything in the nature of violence, and I could hardly conceive it possible that one of us dozen people in that little room was going to be hanged in five minutes. Calcraft, however, was as quick in his movements as he was noiseless. Scarcely had Müller been placed with his back to Calcraft, and we who had followed him arranged ourselves in a half circle in front of him, than Calcraft had buckled a broad leather belt round Müller's waist. Two small straps, fixed to this belt in the middle of the back, were as rapidly passed round the man's arms, and in a trice his elbows were fixed fast to his sides. Müller clasped his hands in the most natural manner, and in this position they were strapped together by a pair of leather handcuffs. The man was pinioned past redemption; and then began a scene that gave a thorough wrench to my nerves.

Calcraft, still noiseless and unimpassioned, was moving round his victim with ominous precision. The belt was tight, the arms were fixed, the hands clasped, and the whole frame at his mercy. He then removed the necktie, and after that the collar. With gruesome delicacy he tucked both within the waistcoat, and Müller was prepared. 'You may sit down,' said Calcraft quietly, but Müller declined. Cool beyond any one in the room, unless Calcraft excelled him, he stood with his short round neck fully exposed, and well placed on a pair of broad shoulders and a firm, round chest. There was not much need to argue the question as to whether Müller could or could not handle poor old Mr Briggs. Müller was a small man, but he was the personification of strength, and with a jaw that meant dogged, resistless obstinacy of purpose. He did not appear to pay much heed to Dr Cappel, the minister, who spoke to him in the intervals of the pinioning, and he listened, apparently without concern, as the Lutheran became more earnest in his invocation after the preparations were complete.

Calcraft left the room, and we all guessed where he had gone to. It was at that time I felt as if a little more callousness would have served me well. To be a passive spectator at such a scene is not a sedative. The imagination will not leave the bare neck and the pinioned arms. One thinks of the hangman examining his rope and the hinges and bolts, and one feels a terribly eerie feeling creeping over one. I had to take myself seriously in hand, and I had resource to an odd expedient. I ate a piece of biscuit, and the distraction carried me over the horrid interval, which was made all the more impressive by the constant tolling of the bell of St Sepulchre's Church. Presently, to my great relief, Calcraft reappeared, and the action was renewed. Dr Cappel stood aside, and the chaplain of the gaol, Mr Davis, led the way to the scaffold, reading the burial service. The journey was short, and those who remember the old hanging days know that the scaffold was erected outside the gaol in the old Bailey. It was through the doorway, known as the debtor's entrance, that it was approached from the prison, and it was up a flight of about ten steps that Calcraft led Müller.

Mr Davis remained below, his duty ended there; but Dr Cappel followed the hangman and his victim, and I followed Dr Cappel. No one else went up, and it occurred to me that perhaps Mr Jonas, the governor of the gaol, to say nothing of the Sheriffs, regarded my presence on the scaffold as an intrusion; but nothing seemed to me more proper, and I was well repaid for my temerity. I saw the people. Far as the eye could reach, to Ludgate Hill on the one hand and right away to Holborn on the other, the entire space, broad and distant as it was, presented an unbroken mass of human faces – types of every unholy passion that humanity is capable of – a seething sea of hideous brutality, that had been surging over the space the live long night, and was now almost still with expectation. The mouths of the myriad of grimy, yellow faces were open, and all the thousands of eyes were upturned upon the spot where I stood with an intentness that was more appalling to me than the methodical movements of Calcraft and the unimpassioned attitude of Müller. The contrast was marvellous. The hangman was curiously busy. He passed a strap round Müller's legs and buckled it; he put the rope round Müller's neck, and tightened the slip knot just under his right ear; he slipped a noose at the other end of the rope over an iron hook depending from the crossbeam of the scaffold, and last of all he pulled a dirty yellow bag over the man's head to his chin. He then stood aside.

Dr Cappel, the minister, stood close to Müller, with his feet on the very edge of the drop; I stood just behind him, but nearer the outside of the scaffold. The conversation was hurried. On Dr Cappel's part it was earnest and excited, but Müller preserved the same stolid, unimpassioned manner that had characterised his attitude throughout. Calcraft, I noticed, disappeared as soon as they began to speak, and I can see Dr Cappel now leaning forward, with both hands extended, as if to draw Müller's words to him as the drop fell and Müller disappeared. Calcraft had done his work well. One strong convulsion and all was over. But Dr Cappel didn't stay to see this. As soon as he recovered from the surprise and alarm caused by the unexpected fall of the drop he dashed down the stairs with his hands aloft, and shouted as he ran, 'Confessed, confessed, thank God!' After one more look at the crowd, now a roaring tumult swaying to and fro, I followed close at his heels and the whole company pressed round him in the chaplain's room, where he told the story of Müller's last words. Just before Müller dropped to his death, he called out 'Ich habe es getan' (I did it).

It is also worth noting part of the account of the execution from *The Times* of 15 November 1864, which gives a further fascinating insight into the contemporary style of reporting a public execution.

The time has been, and very lately too, when the dress in which a felon died, or even a cast of his distorted features, would have been worth their weight in gold. But nothing of this catering for the wretched curiosity of the gallows is permitted now. In whatever clothes our worst felons die, these whether good or bad are burnt before their burial, so that all that may be called the traces of their crime are destroyed with its perpetrator. There is something as just as it is painful, and as just as it is really useful, in this cold obloquy of human nature against its worst dead. There is a feeling among us all which impels us to reverence the earth in which the bones of our departed kindred rest, but from this last consolation even the nearest and dearest relatives of murderers are debarred. For those that die upon the scaffold, there is no tomb but Newgate – a tomb such as the few who love the felon best can only leave with shuddering hope that it may be forgotten. In Newgate there is no solemnity of burial; it is a mere hurried covering of the body of one who was not fit to live among mankind. So with the corpse of Müller. It had died publicly; the surgeon had certified to its shameful death. Towards the middle of the day the rough deal box which held it was filled with shavings and quicklime, and the warders carried it to the hole where it had to be thrust under the flagstones of a narrow, bleak gaol pathway. There, below the massive cross-barred gratings which almost shut out the light of day – there, where none pass the little hidden grave save those who, like himself, must go over it to their great tomb, the body of Müller rests. In a few days the cruelty and singularity of his great crime will be commemorated by a rough 'M' cut in the gaol stone near his head.

Müller's name lived on, not simply as a notorious murderer but in the style of a hat, for the cut-down version of the top hat favoured by Franz Müller became fashionable and was thereafter referred to as a 'Müller hat' or 'Müller cut downs'.

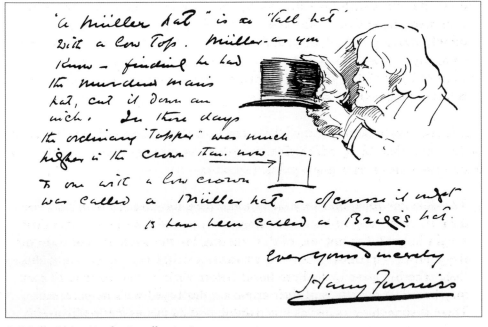

A 'Müller' hat. (*Author's collection*)

4

Undone by a Toy Lantern

MILSOM AND FOWLER AND THE MURDER OF HENRY SMITH

Muswell Hill, 1896

In 1896 the most imposing house in Tetherdown, a thoroughfare leading off Queens Avenue and Fortis Green in Muswell Hill, was Muswell Lodge, sited at what is today the junction of Tetherdown with Burlington Road. This once splendid, but by then decaying, mansion was situated in extensive grounds on the west side of the street. (The land is presently occupied by school buildings and playing fields.) The main entrance in Tetherdown Lane was protected by a high gate and at the rear was a large garden stretching down to Coldfell Woods.

Muswell Lodge was inhabited by 79-year-old retired engineer Henry Smith, a somewhat miserly and reclusive man, who lived alone but was attended by a servant. He had been a widower for twenty-four years. Despite his years, Mr Smith was a strong and remarkably fit man. He was powerfully built, stood 6ft tall and weighed 17 stone. He was also very security conscious and took various precautions regarding the protection of his home. Everywhere was locked at night. His gardener had placed several alarms and mantraps throughout the grounds, and an alarm-gun protected the rear of the premises in case anyone attempted to enter from the woods. A gun was linked to a trip wire that was stretched across the full width of the garden and kept in position about 18in above the ground by a series of iron staves. Anyone coming into contact with the trip wire would fire the gun.

Charles Webber of 1 Coppets Road, Mr Smith's gardener for ten years, used to start work as soon as it was light during the winter months and finish at 5.30 p.m. On the evening of Thursday 13 February 1896 he set the alarm-gun

Muswell Lodge, Tetherdown, the home of Henry Smith. *(Bruce Castle Museum/Haringey Libraries, Archives and Museum Service)*

and left the garden at his usual time. At 11.30 p.m. he returned to bank-up the greenhouse fire, and let himself in and out by the side gate. Everything seemed perfectly normal and all was quiet in the house, as Mr Smith usually went to bed at around 8 p.m.

On the morning of Friday 14 February Mr Webber arrived at Muswell Lodge and was surprised to find everything locked – Mr Smith was an early riser and usually unlocked the front gate. As was his normal practice, Mr Webber went to deactivate the alarm-gun. After discovering that it had been tampered with, he went to the house and knocked on the front door. He became increasingly concerned when he could get no reply and proceeded to investigate further. When he looked through the kitchen window he saw something lying on the floor but could not make out what it was. At that point he decided to summon help. First he called on Joseph Stanbrook, a nurseryman of 3 Tetherdown. By then the early morning light was waking local residents and some were already out on the streets. Several, including Major George Challen, accompanied Webber and Stanbrook back to Muswell

The murder victim Henry Smith, pictured here at Muswell Lodge in 1883. *(Author's collection)*

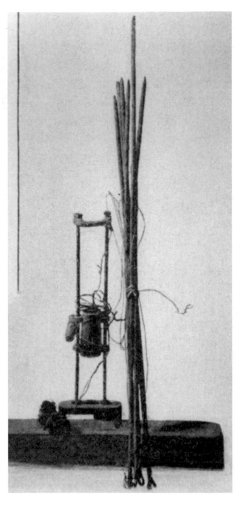

The spring gun. *(Stewart P. Evans)*

Lodge. They found the sash of the kitchen window was up but the blind was down. The major lifted the blind and discovered the body of Mr Smith on the kitchen floor. When they entered the mansion it was clear that Smith had suffered a violent death. Nothing could be done for him and the police were summoned to the murder scene.

The police noted that Henry Smith was dressed in his white nightshirt. His arms had been tied to his body by a tablecloth, which had been torn into strips. His legs were bound in a similar way. Part of the tablecloth and a towel were wrapped around the victim's head, and some of the towel was forced into his mouth. There were bruises to the head and to the hands as well as various cuts. The kitchen showed signs of a violent struggle, there were two separate pools of blood on the floor, and blood was spattered on the walls. The evidence at the crime scene also suggested that Mr Smith had tried to defend himself. A brace and bit had been left on the kitchen table and lying in the sink

THE ESCAPE INTO THE WOODS.

Milsom and Fowler leaving the grounds of Muswell Lodge and escaping in Coldfell Woods early on the morning of 14 February 1896. *(Courtesy of the Campbell Bequest, Hornsey Historical Society)*

they found a small, broken lantern with multicoloured bull's-eye glasses. Two penknives had been left near the body – it was believed they had been used to tear the cloth into strips – and the presence of two knives suggested two people were involved in the crime. Various items of discarded jewellery were found around the house and the still-open safe had been rifled. It was clear to the police that this was a burglary that had gone disastrously wrong. When they examined the grounds they found two sets of footprints near the fence beyond which was Coldfell Woods, clearly the burglars' escape route.

There was extensive press coverage of the case. London's evening papers were the first to break the story when the *Evening News* reported on Friday 14 February, 'Burglary and Murder – old gentleman tied and beaten to death at Muswell Hill'. The following day *The Times*'s headline read: 'Shocking murder at Muswell Hill'. The post-mortem examination on Henry Smith suggested that he had put up a good fight. His injuries were extensive. He had a black eye, about twelve scalp wounds, cuts to both his hands and a broken finger. His skull had also been fractured. The injuries suggested that Mr Smith's assailant had beaten him with a jemmy. The cause of death was given as concussion and loss of blood.

On Wednesday 19 February the *Evening News* reported: 'The funeral of Mr Henry Smith, the old gentleman murdered at Muswell Lodge, took place at noon to-day in the Old Cemetery, Highgate. The remains were buried in a private grave, in which are buried his father and mother and his wife, whom he lost twenty years ago after only eighteen months' happyness [*sic*] of wedded life.' The report went on to say, 'The bearers were eight in number, the coffin being an exceedingly large and heavy one.'

The police acted on the premise that they were looking for two men, and the behaviour of two known felons immediately following the crime left the police with few doubts that the pair were indeed the suspects they were looking for. Albert Milsom was 32 years old and had already been convicted of a long list of crimes, mostly burglary. He used several aliases including Charles Wilson, James Mead and Charles Smith. He was 5ft 6in tall, had dark brown hair, hazel eyes, a dark complexion and muscular build. He was not by nature a violent man. He, his 25-year-old wife Emily and their two children lived at Emily's mother's house at 133 Southam Street, Kensal Town, an area to the north-east of Kensington and west of Maida Vale, straddling Harrow Road. Emily's 15-year-old brother Henry Miller also lived in the house.

Milsom had for some time been associated with another burglar and resident of Kensal Town who also had a long record, but unlike Milsom this man was known to be extremely violent. Henry Fowler, known as Bunny to his friends, was 31 years old, and he too used various aliases, including Henry Sabard and Thomas Brown. He was a powerfully built brute of a man and stood 5ft 10in tall. He had dark hair, brown eyes and a mole just above his left nostril. He was released from Dartmoor on parole on 16 January 1896, having served time for burglary with violence, and was shortly thereafter seen around Kensal Town and Kilburn with Albert Milsom. Unbeknown to Fowler, shortly after his release on licence from Dartmoor a plain-clothes policeman, PC Burrell of the North Kensington force, had been assigned to keep an eye on him. Milsom's renewed association with Fowler had been noted by Burrell.

After their arrest in Bath on Saturday 10 April, almost eight weeks after the murder, Milsom, aware of the mounting evidence against them, gave his account of events to the police, and much of what follows draws on that statement. He said that at about 8 o'clock on the evening of Thursday 13 February, Fowler arrived at his home in Kensal Town and suggested that they do a burglary together. Milsom reported that Fowler said to him, 'I have had a look round with another man who done a lagging with me, and he pointed out several places. There is one place especially where an old man lives. You know how them people are. Any little hole or corner they put their money in. We might find something there. Will you come?'

Milsom said that he refused at first, but Fowler persisted in trying to persuade him and in the end he agreed. Fowler said he needed a light. After asking for a candle and being told none was available, he spotted a small lantern on the kitchen dresser. It had three glasses – white, green and red – and was similar to those used by railway guards. In fact it was a toy lantern which belonged to Milsom's brother-in-law Henry. 'We will take that. It won't throw the reflection so,' said Fowler. The two men went to Kilburn where they drank in a pub with several of Fowler's friends. They then travelled to Muswell Hill, but not before stopping off at another pub. When the two burglars arrived at Muswell Lodge Fowler climbed over the front gate and Milsom followed him. Fowler warned Milsom to look out for any alarms 'or we shall find ourselves being surrounded by police'. They then went around to the back of the house where there was a large lawn with a bed in the centre containing shrubs. They lay in the bushes for about an hour, watching and listening for any movement within the house. Satisfied that all was well, Fowler whispered to Milsom, 'We will get to work.'

Milsom told the police that they then began to search for a way into the house. The drawing-room window was first tried but despite Fowler putting all his weight on the jemmy he had placed under the sash, it would not budge. Next a small scullery window was tried but that was securely barred. They then tried another window, having first removed the flowerpots from the sill. This time Fowler was successful. He opened the sash, then climbed inside the house. The room was a kitchen. Fowler went to the door that led to the rest of the house. Finding it locked he took out a brace and bit from the bag he was carrying and began drilling holes around the lock. Unbeknown to Fowler and Milsom, Henry Smith's bedroom was directly above the kitchen. Mr Smith must have heard either Fowler gaining entry or the vibration of the drill because he went to investigate.

Fowler had drilled two holes through the door and was about to start on a third when Milsom warned him that a light was showing under the door and growing brighter: someone was coming down the stairs. Milsom called to Fowler, 'Bunny, out you come, there's someone coming.' But Fowler did not come out of the window. The two men heard a key being turned in the lock, and Milsom told the police that at this point he ran to the gate to make his escape, expecting that Fowler would be close behind. Next he heard shouts of 'Police! Murder!' He stood by the gate and was surprised and relieved to see no lights or sounds of movement. Having waited a few moments, he then checked the coast was clear before returning to the house. When he reached Muswell Lodge, Fowler stood by the back door covered in blood.

According to Milsom an angry exchange followed: Fowler blamed Milsom for having left him and cited this as the cause of his attacking Mr Smith. Milsom said Fowler was so angry he was afraid the man would turn his violence on him. Fowler eventually calmed down and, leaving Milsom downstairs, went upstairs to see what he could find. He returned with a watch and chain and some jewellery. However, he decided to leave the jewellery behind 'in case of detection'. He had found a key to the safe in Mr Smith's trouser pocket. The safe was opened and rifled. They then left the house and buried their bag of tools in the shrubbery, leaving by the back way and clambering over the fence and into the woods. They decided to wait in the woods until dawn because Fowler's bloodstained clothes might easily be spotted by police patrols. Three or four hours later they made their way back to the road, emerging from the woods at about 6 o'clock into Tetherdown Lane some way from Muswell Lodge. They then set off for Kensal Town, Fowler wearing Milsom's coat to hide his bloodstained clothing.

When they were almost home Fowler announced that he would go to his brother's place for breakfast and would see him again in a couple of hours. When Milsom arrived home he went straight to bed. At about 10 o'clock

The 'relics of the crime'. *(Stewart P. Evans)*

Fowler arrived carrying a parcel containing new clothes. Emily Milsom left the room so he could change into them. He then gave Albert Milsom £50 and said, 'That's more than some would give you after leaving a man in a hole.' Shortly afterwards Fowler went away, leaving his clothes behind for Emily to dispose of. The following day, Saturday 15 February, Milsom took Emily and her brother Henry Miller to Harrow Road, where he bought some new clothes for himself. Milsom paid in gold. Henry carried the clothes home for his brother-in law and en route they stopped off to buy an outfit for Emily.

On returning to 133 Southam Street, Milsom changed into his new clothes and gave some of his old ones to Henry. When Henry noticed that his lantern had disappeared from the kitchen dresser, he complained bitterly. Milsom told him, 'If anybody asks you about the lantern you are to say you broke it and threw it in the dust-hole. It pretty nigh caught us in the fire.' That evening Albert and Emily Milsom went with Henry Fowler and a lady-friend of his to a concert at a public house in Kilburn. They stayed there until after midnight and Fowler, much the worse for drink, became violent. He was argumentative, picked a quarrel with the woman, punched her and knocked her down. With some difficulty Milsom managed to get a cab and they all returned to Kensal Town where the two couples parted.

On Sunday 16 February Milsom left home in the morning after telling his wife he would be back for dinner. He went to meet Fowler who told him, 'I'm off. I have got to show myself on the 16th and I don't intend to give my face away.' Fowler was on parole. His licence required him to visit the police once a month and that very day he needed to report or he would be returned to prison. Fowler was concerned that he might be on the list of possible suspects for the Muswell Hill murder and was not prepared to take the risk of turning up at the police station only to be arrested. Milsom was also fearful that the police were already hot on their trail. Fowler asked Milsom, 'Will you come abroad?' and Milsom, as he later told police, replied in the affirmative.

The two men travelled to the East End where they called on Milsom's aunt, Mrs Waddell, at 62 St Peter's Street, Mile End. Milsom introduced Fowler to her as Mr Jarvis. Having dined at Mrs Waddell's, Milsom told his aunt he had called on her to say goodbye as he was going abroad. Milsom arranged for his mother, his wife and children to visit him at Mile End. Having promised to write soon, he and Fowler travelled to Euston where they caught a train to Liverpool.

Because the pair had frequently been seen together around Kensal Town and Kilburn since January, their sudden flight attracted even more attention and fleeing was probably their biggest mistake. They certainly did not possess the nous to escape detection for long, and their sudden affluence and unfettered, indiscreet spending power had been noted. Fowler's failure to observe the conditions of his licence on 16 February threw further suspicion on him.

While the police investigation into their involvement in the crime was still in its early stages, Milsom and Fowler found lodgings in Liverpool. Milsom wrote to Emily to let her know where he was staying. She sent him a telegram by return informing him that his brother Fred would visit him in Liverpool the following day. Fred handed his brother a sealed letter from Emily which told him that the police had visited their house and were looking for Fowler because he was wanted under the terms of his licence. She also told him that the police knew they had gone off together and that he would get twelve months for being in Fowler's company. At this stage Emily was not aware of any connection between her husband's disappearance with Fowler and the police investigation into the robbery and murder at Muswell Hill.

Fred returned to London and the pair of villains remained in Liverpool. Fowler took one step to try to alter his appearance during his stay there. He had some front teeth missing and this fact appeared in the official police description, so he went to a dentist and had false ones fitted.

Police investigations soon revealed that two men answering the description of Milsom and Fowler had been seen at Euston. A further visit by the police to Milsom's house in Southam Street, Kensal Town, left no doubt that Milsom and Fowler were the men involved in the Muswell Lodge murder and efforts to find them increased. Officers questioned Emily's brother, Henry Miller. He talked quite freely and told the truth. When he was shown the lantern that had been left at the scene of the crime, Henry identified it as his own. Indeed he went to great lengths to explain how several marks had appeared on it. He said he had purchased it at the post office in Golborne Road, Kensal Town, shortly before Christmas 1895. He found it did not work properly, so he repaired it himself. The repairs were clearly visible. Henry explained with enthusiasm the modifications he had made and when the lamp was examined his assertions were easily verified by the police, leaving no doubt that this was indeed his lamp. This was to be the most important and damning piece of evidence against Milsom and Fowler.

Henry told the police that the lantern had disappeared on the night of 13 February, and during his long statement he mentioned that his brother-in-law had woken him as he returned home in the early hours of the following day. Having established this important fact, Chief Inspector Marshall conducted a thorough search of the house. He found some pawn tickets in a teapot. When the items on pawn were redeemed they included a bundle of clothing – Emily had pawned the old clothes Fowler had given her to dispose of and these were the clothes he had worn on the night of the burglary. Among them was a bloodstained jacket. (Proceedings were not taken against Emily: it was decided shortly before the trial of her husband and Henry Fowler that she would not have pawned the bundle of clothes and left the pawn ticket in a teapot where anyone could find it had she been aware of their recent history.)

The police were soon hot on the trail of the two men and only just missed them in Liverpool. Fowler, true to his usual form, had proved objectionable to their landlady by taking a woman back to his room. An argument ensued and the result was that they were thrown out of their lodgings. Milsom and Fowler spent a night in a hotel before leaving for Cardiff, hoping to secure a passage abroad from there. It proved to be a shrewd move as the police were thrown completely off the scent, but Milsom and Fowler never made their journey overseas. It was during their stay in Cardiff that an opportunity arose that may explain why they decided to remain. They encountered a showman, in fact a phrenologist – a person who claimed to be able to read a person's character simply by feeling the bumps on their head. This type of act was a very popular attraction at sideshows, particularly in seaside resorts. He billed himself as 'Professor Sinclair, the Eminent Phrenologist'. Somehow an idea was formulated and Milsom and Fowler, calling themselves Arthur Scott and Harry Taylor, told the professor that they had recently returned from abroad and were looking for a business opportunity to invest in. The idea of some sort of travelling show was discussed.

For a time Fowler remained on his best behaviour. The professor's run came to an abrupt end in Cardiff. The act was paid off two weeks before the end of the show's projected run as a result of lack of an audience and suggestions of chicanery, but not before Milsom and Fowler had assisted the professor and his wife in the various acts they performed, which included ventriloquism. They clearly felt that this was a way they could make some money and escape detection. It was agreed that if the professor could find another venue, they would split the costs and eventually share the profits. After just four days in Cardiff, Milsom and Fowler, along with Fowler's new lady-friend, followed Professor Sinclair to Newport, Pontypool and on to Bristol, where the woman left. The travelling show stayed for two weeks in Bristol and one Sunday during this period Milsom went to London to see his wife and children. He returned to the West Country the following day, bringing his family with him. On 30 March the travelling show moved to Swindon. It had proved an expensive enterprise and the pair of would-be impresarios found themselves covering not only their own expenses but the Sinclairs' also. As was established during the trial, the money rapidly began to run out and so did Fowler's patience and good humour. His grandiose idea of becoming a strongman in the show had not come to fruition and he soon became abusive and threatening towards Professor and Mrs Sinclair.

In Swindon Milsom and Fowler made a failed attempt at breaking into a jeweller's shop. On Sunday 5 April, now desperately short of money, they found themselves in Chippenham where they spent the night in the station waiting-room. The following day they moved to Bath, where they lodged near the theatre above a confectionery and grocery shop kept by Emma Warren at

36 Monmouth Street. Milsom, Emily, their two small children and the Sinclairs all shared one room; Fowler found lodgings elsewhere.

PC Burrell had been hard at work since the disappearance of the two burglars on 16 February. The absence of Emily and her children did not go unnoticed, arousing suspicion that they had joined Milsom. After their departure PC Burrell visited 133 Southam Street and there he discovered an envelope. The postmark enabled him eventually to track the party down. Burrell's investigations took him from town to town, and once he had discovered the existence of Professor Sinclair's travelling show and Milsom and Fowler's involvement in it, his task of discovering their whereabouts became much easier. When the show arrived in Bath on 6 April, Easter Monday, little did the pair know that the police had at last caught up with them.

Once more Milsom and Fowler decided to line up a job. To that end they selected yet another jeweller's, Mr Veal's at 6a Stall Street. While Milsom and Fowler were watching the shop, taking careful note of Mr Veal's movements, the police were watching Milsom and Fowler. On Saturday 10 April two police officers, Chief Inspector Marshall of Scotland Yard and Inspector Nutkins of Kensal Town, travelled to Bath where they joined PC Burrell. A lengthy conference was held with senior local police officers and a plan of action formulated. The following evening the police threw a tight but unobtrusive cordon around 36 Monmouth Street. The officers were given instructions to allow anyone in but nobody out. That evening Milsom was with his wife in their room. At about 11 p.m. Fowler arrived. The police were ready to make their move. The raiding party was unusual in that it consisted principally of senior officers – Chief Inspector Marshall, Chief Inspector Noble, Detective Inspector Mountfield, Inspector Newport, Inspector Nutkins and PC Burrell. All carried loaded revolvers.

When the policemen burst into the room they had the advantage of complete surprise. Each officer had been assigned his man and made for him. Inspector Newport rushed for Fowler who resisted and reached for a revolver which was on the mantelpiece. Chief Inspector Marshall was quick to act and brought the butt of his revolver down on the back of Fowler's head. Milsom was apprehended by Inspector Nutkins; he offered no resistance. Everyone in the room was taken into custody. Milsom and Fowler were both charged with murder, Emily Milsom with being an accessory after the fact. It became clear that Professor and Mrs Sinclair knew nothing about the real identities of the two men and they were released the following afternoon.

Some of Milsom's account of the events may have been true, but his claim that he knew nothing of the planned burglary until 13 February is difficult to believe – several residents of Tetherdown claimed to have seen both Milsom and Fowler acting suspiciously in the area days before the burglary took place. In addition, his account of the crime scene is not entirely consistent with the police evidence. However, the evidence against Milsom and Fowler was so overwhelming that if Milsom did put a slant on the story in his favour it can hardly have altered the outcome of the trial.

Following their arrest in Bath the prisoners were conveyed to the railway station and placed in a sealed compartment with a police escort. When they

The Penny Illustrated Paper, 18 April 1896. *(Hornsey Historical Society)*

arrived at Paddington a large crowd was waiting for them. A crowd had also gathered at Highgate police station where the pair were taken immediately after their arrival in London and formally charged. It became clear during their various appearances at Highgate magistrates' court that the police had gathered a considerable amount of evidence against the two men. It was at this point that Milsom, who was being held in Holloway Prison, wrote to Chief Inspector Marshall offering to confess. Marshall, accompanied by Inspector Nutkins, went to see Milsom on 28 April at Holloway where they heard his lengthy confession. As well as giving a full account of the events, Milsom told the police where he and Fowler had buried their burglars' tools. These were soon found, just as Milsom had said they would be, in the shrubbery in the back garden at Muswell Lodge.

When Fowler heard of Milsom's confession he, too, decided to tell his version of events. Evidence later presented in court recorded that he told a police escort:

My pal, the dirty dog, has turned Queen's evidence and our mouthpiece is no use. But I can tell a tale as well as he. There was £112 in the bag in the safe and I gave him £53 and some shillings which was an equal share of the money after what I had spent. Is it likely that I should give that to a man who stood outside? He put his foot on the old man's neck until he was sure he was dead and then we went upstairs, he first, and found the old man's trousers with the keys of the safe in the pocket. But thieves will cut one another's throats for half a loaf.

The trial of Albert Milsom and Henry Fowler began on 19 May 1896 before Mr Justice Hawkins. C.F. Gill and Horace Avory appeared for the Crown; Milsom was defended by Mr Hutton and Mr Rooth, and Fowler by Mr Woodfall and Mr Abinger. The evidence was heavily stacked against them. In addition to the clue provided by the toy lantern this case is notable for the violent outburst that came as the jury returned with their guilty verdict. Fowler flung himself across the dock at his accomplice and tried to strangle him, very nearly succeeding in saving the executioner the job of hanging Milsom.

Milsom and Fowler received their sentence of death on 21 May. Both were found to be equally guilty of the crime, although doubts were subsequently expressed about the part Milsom played in the slaying of Henry Smith. He was not a violent man but he was easily led, and in the end that was his downfall. The pair were hanged at Newgate on 10 June with a Whitechapel murderer called William Seaman between them. Seaman (in some accounts his name is spelled Seamen) was convicted of the double murder of 77-year-old John Goodman Levy and his 35-year-old housekeeper, Sarah Gale, at 31 Turner Street in 1896. Seaman's last words are reputed to be, 'This is the

Fowler attacking Milsom in the dock at the Old Bailey as depicted in the *Daily Graphic* on Friday 22 May 1896. *(Bruce Castle Museum/ Haringey Libraries, Archives and Museum Service)*

THE DAILY GRAPHIC, FRIDAY, MAY 22, 1896.

first time I've ever been a bloody peacemaker.' The hanging of Milsom, Fowler and Seaman was the last triple execution at Newgate.

On Wednesday 10 June 1896 *The Times* reported:

After hanging an hour the bodies were cut down, and an inquest was subsequently held before Mr S.F. Langham, the coroner of the City of London, at the Sessions-house, in the Old Bailey. The jury, after being sworn, were taken to view the bodies, which were laid out in black coffins in the execution shed. On their way the jurymen had to pass through the corridor in which are buried the bodies of persons previously executed in the gaol, and it was noticed that men were already at work digging the grave which was to receive the bodies of the three culprits. Beyond the marks around the necks caused by the ropes, the corpses of the men presented no indication of the manner of their death. Formal evidence was given by Colonel Milman and Dr Scott, the latter stating that the executions had been carried out satisfactorily, death being instantaneous. The jury returned the usual verdict. The bodies of the men were afterwards buried together in the same grave.

When Newgate was demolished in 1902 the triple scaffold was moved to Pentonville Prison.

5

The First Murderer Caught by Wireless

THE CASE OF DR CRIPPEN

Holloway, 1910

Having discovered that both her family name, which was of Polish origin, and her first name, which was equally difficult to pronounce, were hindering her advancement, Miss Kunigunde Mackamotzki of Brooklyn, New York, took a step which was to have far-reaching consequences. She decided at the age of 17 in 1889 to change her name to Cora Turner. Not long afterwards she was offered a job as secretary to a Brooklyn physician. The buxom young woman soon caught the eye of a professional colleague of her employers: his name was Dr Hawley Harvey Crippen.

Dr Crippen was born in Coldwater, Michigan, in 1862. His father was a dry-goods merchant. He married his first wife, Charlotte Bell, in 1887 in Santiago. The following year a son was born, Otto Hawley Crippen, who was living in Los Angeles at the time of his father's trial in 1910. When Crippen met his future second wife he was a widower – Charlotte had died of tuberculosis about a year before.

Crippen stood 5ft 4in tall; he had piercing blue-grey eyes, which bulged slightly due to an affliction. Compelled to wear thick-lensed glasses, he blinked constantly. When he first saw olive-skinned brunette Cora Turner he was smitten and she evidently saw some potential in the quietly spoken doctor. Cora had already been the mistress of a wealthy stove manufacturer named C.C. Lincoln, and she needed someone who could keep her in the style to which she felt she was entitled. Cora set her sights on the doctor and she was sufficiently alluring to make him forget his loss. They married on 1 September 1892, three months after they had met. Crippen and his new bride went to

Dr Hawley Harvey Crippen.
(Author's collection)

St Louis, where they stayed for about a year. Afterwards they set up house in Brooklyn.

Cora Crippen had aspirations to become a great opera star but it seems these aspirations far exceeded her talent as a singer. Her voice, a thin soprano, was described by one commentator, Filson Young, as 'small but of a clear quality'. Her speaking voice apparently matched her personality: it had an unmistakable New York twang, was loud, vulgar, unsubtle and 'lacking in feminine charm', but the many friends she later made in England spoke highly of her.

At Crippen's trial Dr John H. Burroughs, honorary physician to the Music Hall Ladies' Guild, who first met the Crippens in 1902, described her as 'a vivacious woman, I should say about thirty years of age, bright and cheerful, a very pleasant woman generally'. Cora had every confidence in her abilities as a performer. She was determined to be a success and practised scales day and night – this was where Crippen's troubles began. Evidence in his own account of their relationship and reports proffered by friends, family and acquaintances indicates that following their marriage Crippen lavished attention on Cora and out of love resolved to do everything he could to further his wife's musical ambitions. Crippen was soon spending large amounts on vocal coaches, and promises of work by theatrical agents spurred Cora on.

After two years or so of paying out large sums the doctor began to find the rising costs of financing his wife's 'career' (she had still to earn her first pay cheque as a singer) a heavy burden. He did not want to dampen her enthusiasm, but her efforts to become a great opera star were emptying his pockets faster than he could fill them. A move from New York seemed to provide the answer. Having secured a job as a medical expert for a patent medicine company in St Louis, he probably hoped that in Missouri, away from the bright lights of New York, his wife's enthusiasm for a musical career would wane:

but it did not. Bills from vocal coaches were soon being presented and in St Louis Cora went a step further than she had in New York, having lavish gowns created by expensive costumiers. With increasing costs depleting his finances, Crippen felt obliged to move on and shifted his base of operations. He met with more success in Toronto, Salt Lake City and Philadelphia.

Early in the marriage Cora Crippen had undergone an ovariectomy, so was unable to have children. At 28 and yet to appear on the professional stage, she was beginning to show signs of the character traits that would become the mainstay of her future married life with Crippen. She became frustrated and the once outwardly loving wife began to quarrel with her husband, to criticise and find fault with him at every opportunity. Filson Young, who compiled the Crippen volume for the well-respected *Notable British Trials* series in 1920, said that at this stage the doctor was undoubtedly still fond of his wife, kind to her, patient with her extravagances and the 'interminable calls which she made upon his time and his means'.

At this time Cora decided to change her name again and for her first professional engagement on the stage she became Macka Motzki – unfortunately, her ballooning figure led to her being dubbed 'the Brooklyn Matzos Ball'. Her first stage name was short lived and she soon changed it to Belle Elmore.

When an offer came Dr Crippen's way in 1898, he was overjoyed at the exciting new prospects before him. He jumped at the chance of moving to London for Munyon's Remedies, another patent medicine outfit, on a salary of £3 a week plus commission. Crippen travelled to London in April. In August his wife joined him in rooms in South Crescent. They later moved to Guildford Street before settling at 37 Store Street off Tottenham Court Road, Bloomsbury. Doctor in name only, his professional qualifications did not allow him to practise in England, so he knuckled down to work that amounted to little more than being a salesman. However, his wife had other things to concern herself with; she felt sure that music hall would give her the chance she needed to shine, and she threw herself into her quest. However, Belle Elmore never achieved more than the occasional music-hall or smoking-concert engagement.

She did, however, secure some periods of regular employment, which meant that sometimes she was away from home for short periods or even several weeks. At some of her last appearances on stage during an artistes' strike at the Bedford Music Hall, Camden Town, and the Euston Palace, she was hissed and booed off stage for being a blackleg. On the same bill at the Euston Palace was an actor named Weldon Atherstone, who received a similar reception and was able to sympathise with the weeping Belle. Three years later, in July 1910, in the same week that Belle Elmore's remains were found at Hilldrop Crescent, Atherstone was found shot in the garden of his flat in Battersea. The coincidence was commented upon by Dr Dartford Thomas, the coroner, who a week later was himself dead.

Belle Elmore in one of her many music-hall costumes. *(The Raymond Mander & Joe Mitchenson Theatre Collection)*

Cora Crippen in her stage persona of Belle Elmore. *(The Raymond Mander & Joe Mitchenson Theatre Collection)*

It seems Cora Crippen could not come to terms with the fact that, far from being on the road to becoming a great opera star, her own abilities meant she would not even gain entry into the chorus. Her frustration knew no bounds and evidence suggests that at this point she began to shut her husband out when it came to activities in the bedroom. As Dr Crippen later commented, 'She no longer cared for me.'

Crippen was called to Philadelphia for six months on business and during his absence Cora allowed American performer and ex-prizefighter Bruce Miller into her bed. Then in September 1905 the Crippens moved from their one-bedroom flat in Store Street to a large, semi-detached house in Holloway, North London. Number 39 Hilldrop Crescent was rented for £52 10s a year from Frederick Lown of 12 Ashbrook Road, Highgate.

Situated off Camden Road, Hilldrop Crescent is just a few hundred yards from Holloway Prison and less than a mile from Pentonville Prison, which was to feature significantly in the Crippen case. To supplement their income the Crippens took in paying guests, first German students, then mostly theatricals and variety artistes. This gave Cora the money she needed for her lavish costumes and blonde wigs. Too lazy and grandiose to look after the boarders herself and too mean to employ a maid for the purpose (although the Crippens made use of a charlady occasionally), Cora insisted that her husband get up at the crack of dawn to do the chores. Before he went to his office Crippen would go to the kitchen, take up the ashes, black the fire-grate, then light the fire. He made the tea, cooked the breakfast and polished the paying guests' boots. Reports say that Cora behaved abominably towards her husband,

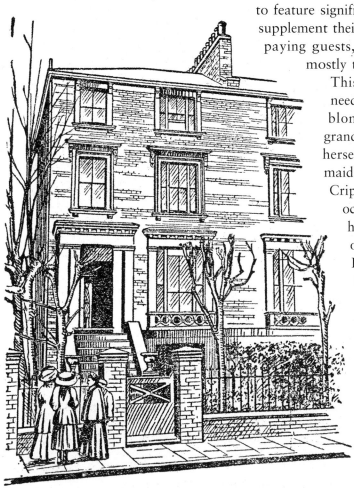

THE HOUSE IN WHICH THE REMAINS WERE FOUND.

Hilldrop Crescent. *(Author's collection)*

A present-day view of Hilldrop Crescent. Margaret Bondfield House stands on the site of Nos 39 and 40. No. 41, seen here on the right, is built in the same style as Crippen's house, which was damaged by German bombs in 1940. *(Paul T. Langley Welch)*

belittling him in front of the lodgers and flirting lasciviously with other men, some of whom she took to her bed. She even chose her husband's clothes for him, right down to his underwear. (One delivery of clothing to the Crippens' household in January 1909 was carefully documented. Jones Brothers of Holloway delivered three suits of pyjamas to 39 Hilldrop Crescent. They were to figure prominently in the events that followed.)

Belle Elmore might not have achieved the degree of success she had hoped for on the stage, but in off-stage theatrical activities she was becoming something of a personality. She was appointed Honorary Treasurer of the Music Hall Ladies' Guild. However, her constant entertaining and her expensive tastes in gowns were a further drain on the Crippens' finances. She was particularly adamant in the choice of colours for both her clothes and the decor of their home. She hated the colour green and considered it unlucky, which was not unusual in theatrical circles. However, her dislike went a step further than theatrical superstition. If she were invited into a room decorated green, she invariably made an excuse and left. Pink was her 'lucky' colour and many of the rooms in Hilldrop Crescent were not only decorated but also draped and upholstered in it.

Some of the most famous music-hall artistes of the day often visited Belle and her husband at Hilldrop Crescent, including Marie Lloyd, the idol of

British music-hall audiences. She referred to Crippen as 'the half a crown king' because he habitually invited people out for a drink and then conveniently remembered he had come out without any money. Vesta Tilley, the celebrated beauty who was best known for her male impersonations, was also a regular visitor.

It seems Crippen was now expected to act as stand-in whenever his wife was without an admirer, and it has been suggested that he took to staying her passion with hyoscine, a poisonous drug used as a nerve depressant and hypnotic. However, on the top floor of his home in Hilldrop Crescent the doctor created a peaceful haven to which he could retreat. He would occasionally relax over a drink in the Admiral Mann pub in nearby Hargrave Place. He didn't smoke because it made him ill, and wines and spirits affected his heart and digestion, but he was a moderate drinker and enjoyed light ale and stout. In his study or den he would read, write and relax during the precious moments he could escape from the hustle and bustle elsewhere in the house.

It may be that at this time he became interested in the works of William Le Queux, an English novelist, diplomat and pioneer broadcaster who specialised in writing mysteries. The only account of a relationship between the two men comes from Le Queux's own contribution to a book entitled *Famous Crimes of Recent Times* and exactly how much truth lies behind it is a matter of conjecture. He was not called as a witness at the trial and I have been unable to find any reference to him in the extensive files released on the Crippen case in 1986. However, in *Famous Crimes* Le Queux claims that Crippen wrote to him in March 1908 at the Devonshire Club and requested an appointment. He used an assumed name, Dr Adams.

Dear Sir, – I have on several occasions read with interest the novels you have written concerning secret poisoning. I, too, take a great interest in the detection of poisons, and perhaps in some little way my knowledge would be helpful to you. Indeed, I have in my mind a new and exciting plot which you could probably use, and I would much like to meet you and discuss it. If you will kindly make an appointment I shall be delighted to keep it.

Le Queux was due to visit Egypt, but after his return to England some three months later he arranged to see 'Dr Adams' at the Devonshire Club. Crippen apparently poured compliments over the author and eventually got on to the subject of poisons; he asked Le Queux if he could secure him a copy of *Secrets of the State of Venice*, a book on poisons that the novelist had referred to in one of his works. Le Queux told Crippen that he owned a copy, having purchased it in a second-hand bookshop in Stockholm, and would have been happy to lend it, but unfortunately it was in his study in Italy.

Le Queux also wrote in his account of the meeting that Crippen seemed to know by heart the *Manual* by Dr Rudolph August Witthaus, an American toxicologist, whose conclusions were generally accepted as standard.

It was then he unfolded a most ingenious plot for a new novel, which turned on an undiscovered murder. He had weighed every detail and taken every precaution, so that there was no flaw by which the assassin could be traced. The whole story, as he conceived it, was far too grim and ghastly, and I told him so. He laughed. 'You ought to show the public how easy it is for a clever man to commit murder and go scot-free.' We met several times afterwards, and he outlined other plots, all of them dealing with the adventures of a poisoner. A little later I went to live in Italy and our correspondence ceased.

In *Famous Crimes of Recent Times* Le Queux's only other reference to his involvement in the case states, 'About a year afterwards, on July 22nd, 1910, I opened an illustrated paper, and there saw the photograph of the visitor who had called himself Dr Adams. But beneath the picture was the name "Dr Hawley Harvey Crippen", and a warrant was out against him for the murder of his wife.'

Crippen secured two part-time jobs in September 1908 while still continuing his association with Munyon's. Both were paid on a commission basis. One involved the sale of ear trumpets, the other was a contract with a dental company which manufactured false teeth. Yale Tooth Specialists was a large concern with offices in Albion House, 61 New Oxford Street, so he moved there from his premises in Shaftesbury Avenue. A secretary was placed at his disposal. Crippen had met the young lady some time previously when he had been working for the Drouet Institute. Miss Ethel Le Neve originated from Diss in Norfolk, but she completed her education in London when her family moved there. In her own account, *Ethel Le Neve: Her Life Story*, written shortly after her trial and published before Crippen's execution, she recalled:

One of our intimate friends happened to be a short-hand teacher, and it pleased him to give lessons both to my sister and to myself in stenography and typewriting. When my sister was proficient as a shorthand-typist she obtained an engagement at the Drouet Institute. Here I joined her. Very soon afterwards came Dr Crippen, who was fated to influence my life so strangely.

For some reason the doctor took kindly to us, and almost from the first we were good friends. But really he was very considerate to everybody. I quickly discovered that Dr Crippen was leading a somewhat isolated life. I did not know whether he was married or not. Certainly he never spoke about his wife, but one day a friend of his called at the office. My sister and I were taking tea with the doctor, which we ourselves had prepared.

'I wish I had someone to make tea for me,' said the friend. Whereupon the doctor, with his customary geniality, pressed him to stay, and during the chat over the tea-cups mention was made of the doctor's wife.

When the friend had gone my sister asked the doctor whether he was really married. 'It would take the lawyers all their time to find out,' was the mysterious reply. That was all he said.

When my sister left to get married I took her place as Dr Crippen's private secretary. With her departure I felt very lonely. Dr Crippen, too, was very lonely, and our friendship deepened almost inevitably.

Other accounts are vague about Ethel Le Neve's early association with Crippen, but it seems she remained Crippen's secretary at Albion House. She was tiny, dark, attractive, demure and genteel – almost the exact opposite of what Cora Crippen had become. She lived in lodgings at 80 Constantine Road, Hampstead, where her landlady was Mrs Jackson. It seems Miss Le Neve and Dr Crippen found that they were soulmates and fell deeply in love, a love cemented in a series of rooms in cheap hotels around Bloomsbury and King's Cross. The relationship was common knowledge among the Crippens' friends and acquaintances. When Cora found out she was outraged. She ridiculed the relationship just as she had for years ridiculed her husband, cheapening it into something absurd. However, when she found out that Ethel was pregnant, it put an entirely different complexion on the matter. Unable to have children herself, she did not like the idea of another woman bearing her husband's offspring. She threatened to leave Crippen and to live with one of her gentlemen friends. She also threatened to take what she referred to as all 'her' money with her. This much Crippen gave in evidence during his trial. Most of their money, some £600, was held in a joint bank account in the Charing Cross Bank, 128 Bedford Street, Strand. On 15 December 1909 Cora gave twelve months' notice to the bank of the withdrawal of the entire amount, but when Ethel suffered a miscarriage, Cora decided to stay with her husband.

One evening in January 1910 Crippen made a rare appearance at one of Cora's social gatherings. Belle (as she preferred to be called on such occasions) was on good form. Lil Hawthorne, one of her variety-performer friends, was there. She said that Belle took her to one side with Dr Crippen and told her that 'Harvey and I have decided to start life all over again. We've both done things we're sorry for, but that's all in the past, isn't it dear?'

By this point in time Ethel had been Crippen's mistress for three years. She was 27, he was 48. Cora Crippen was 35. On 17 January Crippen went to the chemists Lewis & Burrows at 108 New Oxford Street and asked for five grains of hyoscine hydrobromide. This powerful drug came in the form of small, soluble crystals. Lewis & Burrows did not have such a substantial quantity in stock but told Crippen that they would order it for him from their wholesalers, the British Drug House. Crippen duly placed the order in the name of Munyon's Remedies and recorded the planned use for the drug in the Poison Register as 'homeopathic preparation'.

The last people to see Cora Crippen alive were Mr and Mrs Paul Martinetti. Paul and Clara Martinetti were retired music-hall artistes. They were invited to the house in Hilldrop Crescent on the evening of 31 January 1910, and the little dinner party broke up at about 1.30 a.m. Paul Martinetti was in ill health and on the evening of the dinner party Cora was suffering from a slight cold. As the Martinettis left the house Clara said, 'Don't come down, Belle. You'll catch a cold.' Cora waved them goodbye from an upstairs window. Other than Dr Crippen himself, that was the last time anyone saw Cora alive. By this time the lodgers had left the house and had not been replaced. Crippen called on the Martinettis the following day at their flat in Shaftesbury Avenue to see how Paul was. Their conversation was relayed at the trial: 'How is Belle?' enquired Clara Martinetti. 'Oh, she's all right,' came the reply.

Exactly what happened after the Martinettis left 39 Hilldrop Crescent will never be known. Crippen said that he and Cora had a blazing row after she criticised him for not escorting the ill Paul Martinetti upstairs to the lavatory. During his trial he said that his wife told him, 'This is the finish of it – I won't stand it any longer – I shall leave you tomorrow and you will never hear of me again.' Crippen also told the police that his wife said he should arrange to cover up any scandal with their mutual friends and the Guild the best way he could.

At his trial Crippen denied murdering his wife, and he lied persistently, variously and hopelessly about what had become of her until the day he died. Even after he had been found guilty of murder he never confessed. After the verdict had been pronounced and he had been sentenced to death, he said, 'I still protest my innocence.' However, the evidence against him was overwhelming: the remains found in the cellar at 39 Hilldrop Crescent seemed beyond reasonable doubt to be those of Cora Crippen.

It will never be known whether it was the drug hyoscine that actually killed Cora. The toxicological tests carried out on her remains showed a sufficient amount to have killed her, and poisoning by hyoscine was given as the cause of death. If hyoscine had been administered merely to stifle Cora's sexual appetite, perhaps Crippen accidentally gave her an overdose. Perhaps Cora took the poison herself in the belief that it was a sleeping draught, or perhaps Crippen simply gave his wife the poison disguised in drink or food and waited for it to take effect. Taken orally the hyoscine would have caused delirium, then drowsiness, leading to unconsciousness within an hour, then paralysis

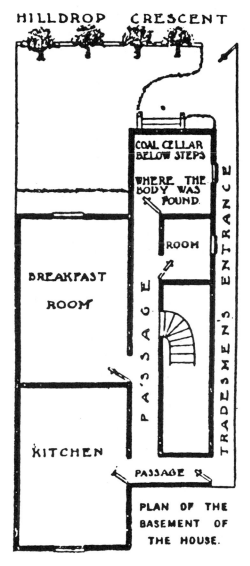

The floor plan of the basement at 39 Hilldrop Crescent. *(Author's collection)*

and within twelve hours, death. The corpse was decapitated, dismembered and filleted. Crippen then set about covering up his wife's disappearance. On the afternoon of 2 February Cora failed to appear at a meeting of the Music Hall Ladies' Guild, held in a room at Albion House. That morning Crippen had gone to his office and dictated two letters which were delivered by hand by Ethel Le Neve, and both were signed 'Belle Elmore'. Neither was in Cora Crippen's handwriting, much to the consternation of the ladies of the Guild. The letters said that she was resigning her membership of the Guild, owing to an urgent visit to America due to a family illness. Cora had apparently been too busy getting ready to go to write the letters herself.

On the day the letters were delivered to the Music Hall Ladies' Guild, Crippen pawned some of his wife's jewellery at Attenborough's of 142 Oxford Street. He did the same on 9 February. The jewellery was pawned for a total of £195, which amounted to more than his annual salary from Munyon's. Lil Hawthorne, Belle Elmore's friend, was on a tour of the provinces when the resignation letter arrived at the Guild. When she returned she wanted more details and went to see Crippen. Hawthorne commented that Belle had left rather suddenly. Crippen informed her that it wasn't a relative of Belle's who was ill but a relative of his. He said the relative lived in San Francisco and that there was quite a lot of money involved, so they had to protect their interests. Naturally one of them had to go and as he couldn't, Belle went instead.

On 26 February Crippen took Ethel Le Neve to the Music Hall Ladies' Guild annual ball at the Criterion – tickets cost half a guinea each. At that point Cora's friends began to take a little more interest in the doctor. Ethel was wearing one of Cora's brooches, something Le Neve mentioned in her account of what happened:

When we had discussed the departure of Belle Elmore the doctor thrust his hand into his pocket and drew out a handful of jewels – the jewels which have figured so much in this case. 'Look here,' he said, 'you had better have these. At all events, I wish you would please me by taking one or two. These are good and I should like to know you had some good jewellery. They will be useful when we are dining out, and you will please me if you will accept them.'

I said, 'Well, if you really wish it, I will have one or two. Pick out which you like. You know my tastes.' Thereupon he picked out a couple of solitaire rings, a ring set with four diamonds and a ruby, and a small diamond brooch – 'the rising sun' brooch. There remained a very large brooch set with beautiful stones in the shape of a tiara, with many rows of diamonds arranged in a crescent, and about half a dozen fine rings.

I think I might say here that Dr Crippen was a real expert in diamonds. He often used to show me how to know the relative values of them by holding them up to the light and watching their colour. As a result I got to know the different fashions of setting, and could distinguish between those set in London and New York.

I then asked what he would do with the remainder, as it would not do to leave them about the house, and as we had no safe, surely it would be better either to sell them or to pawn them. Perhaps the latter course would be best, as he could redeem them whenever he was disposed to do so. 'That is a good idea,' he said. 'I will take your advice.'

It will be seen, therefore, that Dr Crippen pawned the jewels purely on my suggestion. As far as I know, at that time he was not in financial trouble, tempting him to pawn those jewels immediately, as was suggested in court.

Miss Le Neve went on to say:

After all, as regards the jewels, they had been bought by Dr Crippen as an investment. It was impossible for Belle Elmore to have paid for them. I have seen her contracts, and I know that even when engaged on tour her salary amounted at the most to £3 a week, out of which she had to pay her agent's fee and other expenses. How, then, could she have bought jewels worth many hundreds of pounds? And if the property were not hers why should she take it away?

At the ball neither the 'rising sun' brooch nor the relationship between the doctor and his secretary escaped the scandalised eyes and the gossiping tongues of the ladies of the Guild. Belle's friends were puzzled that they hadn't heard from her, not even a postcard. When one committee member of the

Guild, Louise Smythson, asked Crippen for his wife's address he told her that she was 'right up in the wilds of the mountains of California'. She then said to him, 'When you get to hear of her will you let us know?' Crippen answered, 'Yes, when she has a settled address I will let you know.'

On Saturday 12 March 1910 Ethel moved into 39 Hilldrop Crescent, posing as a housekeeper. A French maid was later engaged – they brought her back from France after visiting Boulogne that Whitsuntide. She was called Valentine and was 17 years old.

Mrs Jackson, Ethel's landlady, told the court at Crippen's trial that Le Neve had been 'much depressed and in tears in January'. 'It's Miss Elmore,' Ethel informed Mrs Jackson. 'When I see them go away together it makes me realise what my position is.' Ethel also confided in her landlady, 'She's been threatening to go away and when she does, the doctor's going to divorce her and marry me.' Before leaving her lodgings (she had spent little time there in the preceding weeks) she informed Mrs Jackson that Mrs Crippen had gone to America.

After her arrival at the house in Hilldrop Crescent, Ethel was seen in Holloway and district wearing clothes and furs that had belonged to Cora Crippen. On Wednesday 16 March Crippen gave his landlord three months' notice of his intention to vacate the house. Having still not heard from Belle, her friends asked Crippen for news. He told them his wife had developed pneumonia in California and was dangerously ill. Then on 24 March the doctor and Le Neve went on a five-day Easter holiday to Dieppe as Mr and Mrs Crippen. Before they left Crippen sent a telegram to the Martinettis saying, 'Belle died yesterday at six o'clock. Peter.' (To most of Belle Elmore's theatrical friends her husband was known as Peter – a name she sometimes called him too.) Crippen also took out a death notice in *The Era* on 26 March. Printed on page 17, it simply read:

ELMORE. – March 23, in California, U.S.A.
Miss Belle Elmore (Mrs H.H. Crippen).

The same publication, read widely by music-hall and variety artistes, printed an obituary and details of the case on 23 July.

On their return from France, Crippen continued with his subterfuge as Cora's friends bombarded him with questions. 'She passed on of pneumonia, up in the high mountains of California,' he told them. Requests for details of where flowers could be sent were answered with 'There was no point in sending flowers as the funeral had already taken place.' Crippen said that his wife had been cremated and her ashes would be sent to him in England. He had perhaps underestimated his wife's popularity. Cora's friends would not let the matter rest, particularly when it was discovered that on her arrival in

America she had not made contact with any of her acquaintances in New York. Meanwhile, Crippen continued to administer his business affairs as usual and on 18 June he arranged with his landlord to stay on until 29 September at Hilldrop Crescent.

However, Lil Hawthorne, widely known as a busybody, was not satisfied. She continued to pester Crippen because, she said, she wanted to pay her respects to her dear friend. He told her he was still awaiting Cora's ashes, but she did not believe him. Lil Hawthorne was not the type of woman to be put off easily; she smelled a rat and she was one of the chief instigators of a move to ensure the authorities looked into the situation. A friend of one of the members of the Music Hall Ladies' Guild happened to be Detective Superintendent Froest of Scotland Yard. He was in charge of the recently formed serious crime squad. The suspicion that something was not quite right was communicated to Froest and he promised to look into the matter. Detective Chief Inspector Walter Dew was assigned to make general enquiries.

Dew and Detective Sergeant Mitchell visited 39 Hilldrop Crescent on 8 July. The doctor was not at home; only Ethel and the French maid were at the house. Ethel told the two policemen that Crippen was at his office and she agreed to accompany them to Albion House. When they arrived Dew explained the reason for the visit and Crippen said, 'I suppose I'd better tell the truth,' a quote Dew later reported in his autobiography. A statement was taken over the course of five hours. Crippen said that by the time he came home from work on 1 February his wife had gone. She had run off with another man. To add insult to injury she had left most of her clothes and the jewels he had given her, and left him with no clue as to her whereabouts. Realising she had finally left him he had sat down to think about how he could explain his wife's disappearance without causing a scandal, and conceal the fact that he had been cuckolded.

After the statement had been taken, the doctor and Ethel accompanied the two policemen to Hilldrop Crescent, where Crippen allowed them to look around. They searched the house from top to bottom, including the coal cellar, and were satisfied nothing was amiss. Crippen must have felt uneasy about this police attention, because at this point he panicked and fled with Ethel to Rotterdam.

On Monday 11 July Chief Inspector Dew returned to Albion House to clear up some final points. Crippen was not at his office. However, his associate, Dr Rylance, informed the inspector that on the previous Saturday he had received a letter from Crippen instructing him to wind up his business affairs and household accounts. Included in the letter was the sentence 'In order to escape trouble I shall be obliged to absent myself for a time.' A dental technician employed at Albion House, William Long, told Dew that Crippen had sent him out to purchase clothing for a boy of 16, and he had gone out and bought a brown tweed suit, stockings, boots, hat and overcoat.

When the inspector visited 39 Hilldrop Crescent, he discovered that the only occupant was the French maid, Valentine. It was clear that further investigation would be required. The house was searched from top to bottom once again, and a third time during the 12th and 13th. On first inspection the coal cellar seemed to be perfectly in order. Even after a second inspection, nothing appeared to be amiss. It was only when Dew prodded the cellar floor with a poker that he discovered some of the bricks were loose. Dew and Detective Sergeant Mitchell removed them. There was evidence that the earth beneath had recently been disturbed and the presence of lime encouraged them to dig deeper. It was not long before what little remained of Cora Crippen was found at a depth of 5in. Wrapped in a flannelette pyjama jacket was a stinking mass of human flesh, skin, viscera and hair (some of it attached to a Hinde's curler). There was also part of a tattered handkerchief and a cotton camisole. The remains were subsequently placed in a coffin and removed to Islington mortuary in Holloway Road.

The remains were examined by Dr Pepper, Master in Surgery of London University and a Fellow of the Royal College of Surgeons; Dr Herbert Willcox, senior analyst of the Home Office; and Dr Bernard Spilsbury (later Sir Bernard), pathologist at St Mary's Hospital, Paddington, and a noted witness in several celebrated murder trials. The Crippen case brought Spilsbury to public prominence. The discovery of hyoscine hydrobromide led the pathologists to conclude that poisoning by the same was the cause of death. Hyoscine was sometimes used in a mild form in injections, but taken orally it caused certain death. A quarter of a grain to half a grain of hyoscine constitutes a fatal dose and the traces found in the remains amounted to two-fifths of a grain, which, according to the expert evidence given at Crippen's trial, corresponded to more than half a grain in the whole body. Pepper and Spilsbury concluded that the remains were those of a stout female who bleached her hair. Part of the flesh from the abdomen showed a scar consistent with the ovariectomy undergone by Cora Crippen. Dr Willcox confirmed the presence of hyoscine, corroborating the evidence of Pepper and Spilsbury at the trial.

How did Crippen dispose of his wife's head, limbs and torso bones? There is a commonly held belief that her head was thrown overboard in a large handbag, carpetbag or hatbox during the trip he took to Dieppe with Le Neve. Perhaps as a subtle act of vengeance he burned as much as he could in the fire-grate he had been forced to clean by his domineering wife. This particular method has been cited in several examinations of the case as the means of disposal, but it seems unlikely. The burning of flesh and bones in such large quantities would have created an awful stink in the street outside and for prolonged periods. Too much attention would have been drawn to the house if such a method had been used.

The front page of the *Daily Graphic*, Tuesday 19 July 1910. The individuals featured are:
1. Mr Long, who was asked by Crippen to wind up his household affairs. 2. Paul
Martinetti, who told of the last time he saw Mrs Crippen alive. 3. Dr Marshall, who made
the first examination of the remains. 4. Mrs Martinetti, who corroborated her husband's
evidence. 5. Walter Schroder, the Deputy Coroner. 6. Chief Inspector Walter Dew, who was
in charge of the case for Scotland Yard. 7. Dr Danford Thomas examining the first witness.
[8]. Mr J.E. Nash, who first gave the evidence to the police that led to the discovery of the
crime. *(Author's Collection)*

A warrant was issued on 16 July for the arrest of Crippen and Le Neve for murder and mutilation. The story made headline news. A police description of Crippen read:

Hawley Harvey Crippen: Age 50, 5ft. 3" or 4", complexion fresh, hair light brown, inclined sandy, scanty, bald on top, rather long scanty moustache, somewhat straggly, eyes grey, bridge of nose rather flat, false teeth, medium build, throws his feet outwards when walking. . . . Somewhat slovenly appearance, wears his hat rather at back of head. Very plausible and quiet spoken, remarkably cool and collected demeanour.

As for the doctor and his mistress, while Cora Crippen's remains were being discovered the lovers were in Belgium, staying at the Hotel des Ardennes in Brussels. On Wednesday 20 July, having boarded the SS *Montrose* at Antwerp as Mr John Philo Robinson and Master John Robinson (at this time passports were not required for travel), they set sail for Quebec. They were not aware that the hunt was already on for them. Crippen had shaved off his moustache and removed his metal-rimmed spectacles, but his failure to refrain from being over-affectionate towards the '16-year-old son' with whom he shared Cabin No. 5 aroused the suspicion of Captain Kendall, who clearly fancied himself as something of an amateur sleuth. Kendall noticed that although Mr Robinson did not wear spectacles, red marks on his nose suggested that he had done so until recently. He watched the couple more closely and quickly came to the conclusion that Master Robinson was a woman.

A police notice giving descriptions of Crippen and Le Neve had been given to Kendall at Millwall Docks on 14 July. He bought a copy of the continental edition of the *Daily Mail* on the 20th and it contained pictures of the couple. Having studied Crippen's photograph, and allowing for the lack of spectacles and moustache, he believed that he had found the fugitives and communicated the news to Scotland Yard via the new Marconi Electric Telegraph. The SS *Montrose* was then one of only sixty ships in the world equipped with this device and this was the first time telegraph had ever been used to catch a criminal. The message ran: 'Have reason to believe Dr Crippen and Miss Le Neve are travelling as passengers on my ship. They are posing as father and son and should reach Quebec on July 31. Await instructions. Kendall.' On hearing the news Chief Inspector Dew made arrangements to travel to Quebec by a faster ship, the SS *Laurentic*, which set sail from Liverpool on 23 July and arrived in Quebec ahead of the *Montrose*.

During Inspector Dew's absence police investigations continued in England. On 27 July a statement was taken from Lena Lyons by Sergeant C. Cruchett. It reads:

Statement made by Mrs Lena Lyons of 46 Brecknock Road, N., who says

Between 7 and 8 o'clock one morning in either the latter end of January or the beginning of February last, whilst in bed I distinctly heard the sound of 2 shots. There was an interval of several seconds between each one. It was quite dark at the time and the sound startled me: they came from the direction of 39 Hilldrop Crescent. My lodger who at that time occupied the first floor and slept in the back room, overlooking 39 Hilldrop Crescent, came running down to my room. She said, 'Did you hear that shot Mrs Lyons?' I said, 'Yes', and immediately we heard the second report.

I spoke to Mrs Lowe, the person next door, about it, also to my husband. He said it must have been a motor but I was convinced it was the sound of revolver shots. I only mention [sic] it to my husband and Mrs Lowe as people have spoken of Mrs Glackner of the Oil shop, 30 Brecknock Road, who said she heard screams, as an old gossip.

This statement was corroborated on the same day in an account given by May Pole, Mrs Lyons's lodger.

During the whole of the eleven-day voyage Dr Crippen and Ethel Le Neve were unaware that their deception had been detected. Captain Kendall made full use of the Marconi Electric Telegraph by sending regular reports of the couple's activities. Every morning the *Daily Mail* reported the latest news on the fugitives and their pursuers. On Sunday 31 July the SS *Montrose* steamed slowly up the St Lawrence River towards Quebec. Mr Robinson was on deck, 'Master Robinson' was reading in Cabin No. 5. As Mr Robinson was taking in the sights he noticed a pilot boat approaching. It came alongside and several people boarded the *Montrose*. The party included Chief Inspector Dew, his sergeant and some female wardresses.

Dew went to the bridge to pay his compliments to Captain Kendall. Formalities over, the small party made its way along the deck towards Mr Robinson. As the party drew near, Dew stepped forward and said, 'Good morning, Dr Crippen. I am Chief Inspector Dew of Scotland Yard. You will be arrested.' Crippen was startled at first. He had not recognised Dew immediately because without spectacles his vision was not particularly keen.

Dew originally reported in 1910 that Ethel became 'agitated and fainted'. However, in his autobiography he said, 'With a shriek she collapsed.' Ethel's own account says:

I remember that fateful Sunday morning that Dr Crippen pressed me after breakfast to go on deck with him. 'I don't think I will,' I said. 'It's very wretched up there, and I would rather stay down here and finish this book before lunch.' He went away quietly. Little did I know that I should not speak to him again for many days. A little time passed, and then the blow fell. There was a tap at the cabin door. I turned round quite naturally, expecting to see the doctor again. Instead I saw Inspector Dew! Even in his pilot's garb I did not fail to recognise him instantly.

The sight of him stunned me. At this moment, for the first time, I realised there was something dreadful amiss. That this inspector should have chased us all the way from England filled me with horrible forebodings. I gave a cry, and then fell into a swoon.

When I recovered I heard Inspector Dew read out his warrant for my arrest. I heard something about the 'murder and mutilation' of Mrs Crippen as in a dream. What it meant I did not know.

When he searched Crippen Inspector Dew found two cards. Both had the name 'John Robinson' printed on them and were inscribed in pencil. The first read: 'I cannot stand the horror I go through every night any longer and as I see nothing ahead and money has come to an end, I have made up my mind to jump overboard tonight. I know I have spoiled your life but I'll hope some day you can learn to forgive me. Last words of love. Yours H.' The second card read: 'Shall we wait till tonight about 10 or 11? If not, what time?' Some details concerning these cards came out at the trial when Crippen said that a quartermaster had brought him a letter explaining that he knew his and Miss Le Neve's true identities and that they were to be arrested on arrival in Montreal. The quartermaster agreed to hide Crippen and help fake a suicide. He would go to Captain Kendall in the night and tell him that he had heard a splash. When the cards were found it would be assumed that Crippen had committed suicide. However, Inspector Dew's party boarded the *Montrose* before Crippen had had time to put his plan into action, and once the cards had been found, the doctor was shackled for his own protection.

After being detained in Canada for almost three weeks, Crippen and Le Neve were brought back to England under arrest aboard the SS *Megantic*. Dew travelled as Mr Doyle and Crippen as Mr Nield. Ethel was looked after by wardresses. Crippen had already begun to grow his characteristic moustache again. The couple were not allowed to communicate. In her published account of the story Le Neve said:

The two wardresses who had been sent out to guard me never relaxed their vigilance. At night one of them always sat up with me while the other slept.

Even now I think of one or two amusing incidents which relieved the monotony. Inspector Dew, who was always very kind, used to visit us often, and he was so paternal in his manner that we got accustomed to calling him 'Father'. 'Dear me, "father" is very grand to-night,' we used to say when the inspector put on his evening dress and dined with the general company in the state saloon.

When nearing Ireland we encountered very rough weather, and we all felt the effects of it. Inspector Dew himself fell victim to sea-sickness. On the landing-stage at Liverpool there was so great a crowd that I was nearly lost! The Canadian soldiers who had travelled over with us kept the throng back when it threatened to separate me and the two ward-resses from the detectives who were in front in charge of Dr Crippen.

It was only as I entered the train that I caught a glimpse of the doctor, huddled up between his guards. He looked very wistful, and saddened me. I nodded to him and smiled, just to cheer him up, and his face brightened very much. At Euston there was another very large crowd to witness our arrival. But here, I am glad to say, I was allowed to walk across the platform just like an ordinary passenger to the taxi-cab which was waiting to convey me to the street.

When we reached the police-station we were taken at once into the charge-room. There Dr Crippen and I stood side by side while the same dreadful words about 'murder and mutilation' were read out. The next time I saw the doctor was when we passed into the dock at the police-court to begin the terrible ordeal of a public trial. Even in those painful surroundings it was a comfort to me to be near him again. Now and then we whispered together; but, unfortunately, Dr Crippen is a little deaf in the left ear, and that was nearest to me, so that we could only have a few snatches of conversation.

At the police-court during the week which followed I heard the full details of the discovery at Hilldrop Crescent. All the time the evidence seemed to me utterly unreal and past belief. I could not associate the doctor with cruelty or crime. I knew him only as a man of tenderness and gentle nature, and it is thus that I now think of him.

It was thus that I thought of him when I sat in my lonely cell at the Old Bailey waiting wearily day after day while his trial was going on in the court above.

What little remained of Cora Crippen was interred at Finchley Cemetery on 10 October 1910. The cortège, consisting of a hearse and three mourning coaches, left Leverton's undertakers at 163 York Road, Camden Road, at 3.15 p.m. A few bits of flesh were retained as evidence.

The trial of Dr Crippen began on Tuesday 18 October 1910 at the Old Bailey before the Lord Chief Justice, Lord Alverstone, and lasted for five days. Ethel Le Neve was to be tried separately with being an accessory after the fact. She did not give evidence at her lover's trial because Crippen insisted to his

This Old Bailey, the building familiar to us today, was constructed on the site of Newgate Prison and opened by Edward VII in 1907. This postcard was sent on 18 October 1910 to Sheffield and the message on the back reads: 'I am having a very enjoyable time down here. The weather is splendid. I am going to see Westminster Abbey this afternoon. They say it is splendid inside. This is where Crippen trial is going to be held today.' *(Chris Sharp of Old Barnsley)*

Lord Alverstone, who tried the case. *(Author's collection)*

legal advisers that she should not be called as a witness on his behalf. Richard Muir appeared for the Crown and Crippen's defence was conducted by A.A. Tobin. Tobin contended that there was no proof that the remains in the cellar were those of a woman, let alone those of the doctor's wife. Moreover, it was suggested that the remains had been buried in the cellar at 39 Hilldrop Crescent sometime before September 1905, when the Crippens had moved into the house. However, the telltale label on the pyjama jacket, bearing the words 'Shirtmakers Jones Brothers, (Holloway) Limited, Holloway', proved beyond any reasonable doubt that the remains could have been buried only after the Crippens had moved in, because Jones Brothers did not become a Limited Company until 1906. In addition the cloth from which the pyjama jacket was made 'did not come into existence' until November 1908, and it was proven that both the patterned cloth and the pyjamas were manufactured that same month. Never was circumstantial evidence so purely circumstantial and yet so damning. On the fifth day of the trial, having heard all the evidence, the jury retired and returned after only 27 minutes with a guilty verdict. Sentence of death was pronounced.

The trial of Ethel Le Neve began on 25 October and lasted just one day. She appeared before the same judge and the same prosecutor as her lover. She was defended by F.E. Smith KC, afterwards 1st Earl of Birkenhead. She gave no evidence, but was acquitted and set free. Crippen's appeal was heard on 5 November. It failed.

The execution of Dr Hawley Harvey Crippen took place on the morning of 23 November 1910. The executioner was John Ellis, who was a barber and publican when not engaged on 'government work'. He was held in high regard for his efficiency. After Ellis removed the doctor's spectacles, Crippen made a last request to the prison governor, Major Owen Edward Mytton-Davies, that a photograph of Ethel and her letters be buried with him. He went to his death calmly. Three other men were awaiting execution at Pentonville Prison. In consideration of their feelings, the traditional tolling of the prison bell to signify that an execution had just taken place was dispensed with. The bell was never again tolled to mark an execution. After Crippen had been hanged, two notices were posted on the prison gates. The first was the 'Declaration of the Sheriff and Others', which confirmed that judgement of death had been carried out; the second was the 'Certificate of the Surgeon', which confirmed that the prisoner was dead.

Mr R.D. Muir opening the case for the Crown. *(Author's collection)*

Crippen and Le Neve in the dock. *(Stewart P. Evans)*

A.A. Tobin KC, who defended Crippen. *(Author's collection)*

After Crippen had been pronounced dead, the body was left hanging in the locked execution shed for the customary one hour. Afterwards it was taken to the mortuary for a post-mortem examination and inquest; and shortly after that, around noon, it was buried in the prison yard under 8ft of earth along with a photograph of Ethel Le Neve.

Three hours after Crippen's execution Le Neve set sail aboard the *Majestic*, dressed in mourning, a veil hiding her face. She was entered in the passenger list as 'Miss Allen'. After a very brief stay in New York she travelled to Canada where she settled in Toronto and worked as a typist. Early in 1911, she was granted probate of Crippen's will, valued at £268. Letters of administration

CRIPPEN TO HANG.

CLOSING SCENES OF GREAT MURDER TRIAL.

THE DAILY GRAPHIC, MONDAY, OCTOBER 24, 1910.

CRIPPEN'S FATE.

NOTABLE TRIAL ENDS IN SENTENCE OF DEATH.

IMPRESSIVE SCENE.

Dr. Crippen was convicted of the murder of his wife, and sentenced to death at the Old Bailey on Saturday. Our special representative describes the scene in this column. Mr. Muir's address to the jury and the Lord Chief Justice's summing-up appear on page 10.

(BY OUR SPECIAL REPRESENTATIVE.)

It is seventeen minutes to three, and the jury have been absent for twenty-eight minutes. An usher enters carrying the terrible exhibits which have been examined by the jury in their retiring-room. So we know that the jury have considered their verdict and arrived at a decision. So we know that the fate of Dr. Crippen is settled, that the question of life or death has been decided for him in twenty-eight minutes! A surprise thrills through the crowded court because an indefinable rumour or belief had been flitting among us suggesting that the jury would have difficulty in agreeing, that perhaps one would prove obdurate and stand out against his fellows. And yet, remembering the summing-up of the Lord Chief Justice, so scrupulously fair and yet so remorselessly logical in its sequences of correlated facts and reasonable inferences, there was actually no reason for surprise. For each man in his heart had condemned the prisoner.

A pale, orange-tinted light floods the court as the jury stumble back into their places, is thrown downwards on the mass of tense, upturned faces from some crevices in the ceiling, and starts strange, fantastic shadows flickering in our midst. The judge, holding up a fold of his deep scarlet gown, enters slowly and resumes his seat.

"Are you agreed upon your verdict, gentlemen?" The foreman of the jury is about to reply, when the judge intervenes.

"We must have the prisoner here," says he.

CRIPPEN'S LAST APPEARANCE.

Yes, it is certainly essential that Dr. Crippen should be present! We hear a patter of light footsteps on the stairs leading up to the dock, and for the last time Dr. Crippen appears in that scene which must be now so familiar to him. He steps up briskly, disdaining the assistance of the banister. He has his black overcoat swung over one arm. He seems quite strong, self-dependent, and without constraint. But he has changed since we first saw him, changed since he stood smiling and chatting in the witness-box. He has grown older;

a look of age has come into his face. It is a parched face, dry and scribbled over and over with new sad lines. His eyes quiver no longer; they have grown steadfast. Always prominent, they now seem to actually bulge against the lenses of his bevelled spectacles. He looks straight at the jury, at each juryman, but it is not a look that could be construed by any flight of imagination into a glance of appeal; it is rather a keen scrutiny. He sits down, inscrutable, cold, self-possessed as ever. If there is a nerve aching in this extraordinary man's little body the only external sign is the twitch and contraction of his thin white hands.

A profound silence fills the court, silence and a sense of unusual doom. A clear, matter-of-fact, business-like voice breaks the silence, the Clerk of Arraigns repeating his question to the jury.

Yes, they are all agreed!

The foreman pauses, grips the ledge of the jury-box, and speaks huskily, with a slow utterance.

"We — find — the—prisoner—guilty—of—wilful—murder."

DOOMED.

Several women present cover their eyes. We hear a sob up in the gallery, where a white handkerchief flutters distinctly. The doomed man rises at a motion from a warder. His face is stained with a grey, leaden colour, and a little nerve works jumpily in his throat. But he finds no difficulty in rising. He even straightens himself into a more soldierly attitude than he has ever presented before. He looks straight before him, and if one can dare to read a definite suggestion in a man's looks at so supremely awful a moment, his hard blue eyes are hot with resentment.

Has he anything to say why sentence of death should not be pronounced upon him?

He pauses and clears his throat, which seems choked. At last he speaks, hoarsely, and in a low, guttural accent.

"I still protest my innocence."

The black cap is placed on the judge's head, and an usher calls through the silence for silence! The judge leans forward with his arms spread out upon the little table before him. He looks steadfastly at the prisoner, and in a strong, earnest voice pronounces the dread sentence of death. He will not dilate upon the ghastly and wicked nature of the crime, but he implores the doomed man to harbour no thoughts of a reprieve, but to make his peace with God.

"Amen."

The word is uttered by the silver-haired priest standing with bowed head near the judge's chair.

Dr. Crippen turns. The warders close in upon him, but he does not need their assistance. He walks steadily towards the stairway and passes for the last time from our sight, still impassive, still extremely calm, still inscrutable!

RANDAL CHARLTON.

An article that appeared in the *Daily Graphic* on Monday 24 October 1910. *(Author's collection)*

The gravestone erected by the Music Hall Ladies' Guild over the remains of Cora Crippen at St Pancras and Islington Cemetery, East Finchley. *(Paul T. Langley Welch)*

regarding Mrs Crippen's estate were granted to Mrs Theresa Hunn (Cora Crippen's sister Tessie). Ethel returned to England in 1914 and worked in London as a typist at Hampton's furniture store in Trafalgar Square under the surname Harvey (Crippen's middle name). It was there that she met her future husband, accountant Stanley Smith from Croydon, who was also employed there. They married and had a son and a daughter. A faded photograph of Stanley Smith in military dress (sergeant's uniform) and their son, evidently taken during the First World War, appears in *The Crippen Files*, compiled by Jonathan Goodman. He had a moustache not unlike Crippen's, and although he had more hair and eyes that were not so bulging, otherwise his physical resemblance to Crippen is quite remarkable. Stanley Smith suffered a heart attack at work shortly before his 70th birthday when he was due to retire.

In 1954 the famous journalist Ursula Bloom discovered Ethel's whereabouts and interviewed her. Faithful to the end, she maintained that Crippen knew nothing about the remains found at Hilldrop Crescent and was innocent of any crime. Ethel lived out the remainder of her life between London and 10 Parkway Road, Addiscombe, in relative obscurity. She died a widow, aged 84, in Dulwich hospital on 9 August 1967. She requested that a gilt locket containing a picture of Dr Crippen which she had held on to through all the years since 1910 should be placed in her coffin.

Crippen's solicitor, Arthur Newton, had been allowed access to Crippen while he was under sentence of death. Following the execution, for financial gain Newton colluded with various newspapers and journals regarding a letter supposedly written by Crippen after the trial, in which he confessed to the murder and mutilation of his wife. Newton knew that this claim was completely untrue. No such letter existed. As a result of his professional misconduct the King's Bench Division of the High Court suspended him for twelve months from 12 July 1911. In 1913 Newton was sentenced to three years' penal servitude for defrauding an Austrian businessman. On his release from Parkhurst, he was struck from the rolls by the Law Society. He became a private investigator and died in 1930.

John Ellis, Crippen's executioner, resigned in 1924. In the course of twenty-three years he had executed 203 men and women. Later that year Ellis tried to

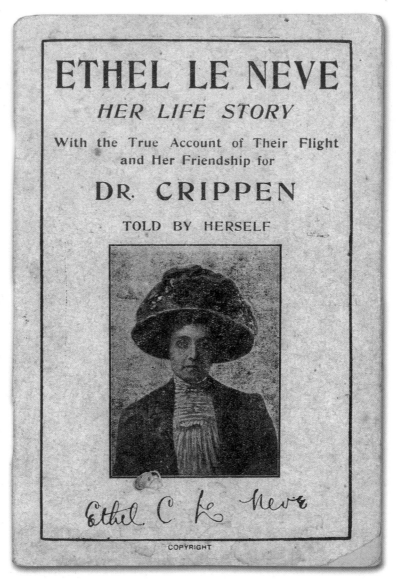

ETHEL LE NEVE

HER LIFE STORY

With the True Account of Their Flight
and Her Friendship for

DR. CRIPPEN

TOLD BY HERSELF

Ethel C Le Neve

COPYRIGHT

The cover of *Ethel Le Neve: Her Life Story. (Edward Black)*

commit suicide. After drinking heavily, he attempted to shoot himself through the head. He bungled it and succeeded only in fracturing his jaw. He appeared before a magistrate who told him, 'I am sorry to see you here, Ellis. I have known you for a long time. If your aim was as true as some of the drops you have given, it would have been a bad job for you.' He was bound over to keep the peace for a year and to stay away from strong drink and thoughts of suicide. Ellis became very depressed. His health was not good and he continued to drink heavily. In September 1932, nine years after he had first attempted suicide, he slit his throat with a cut-throat razor. This time he did not bungle it. He was 58 years of age. The coroner's verdict was 'Suicide while of unsound mind'.

After the trial and execution 39 Hilldrop Crescent was purchased by Scottish comedian Sandy McNab for £500 and opened as a museum of Crippen relics. Public disapproval put an abrupt end to that scheme and it briefly became a boarding-house for theatricals. Between the two world wars the house stood empty. Then in 1940 it was damaged by German bombs. It was demolished after the war and since 1954 the site has been occupied by a block of local authority flats known as Margaret Bondfield House, named after Britain's first woman cabinet minister. Hilldrop Crescent still retains a few of its houses from the time when the Crippens occupied No. 39, the houses which remain being similar in style and proportion to the home of Dr and Mrs Crippen.

Crippen maintained his innocence to the very end. There was no last-minute confession and the evidence against him seemed to prove beyond any reasonable doubt that he killed his wife. However, the case continues to be the focus for reassessment and re-examination and in July 2004 a television programme, *The Last Secret of Dr Crippen*, sought to cast some doubt on the conviction. It was said that two letters written by Cora Crippen from America were sent to Crippen at Pentonville Prison, but neither he nor his solicitors was given sight of them. I have been unable to locate these letters in any of the official files. The first was allegedly posted from Chicago and written the day Crippen was convicted. It was said to have been received by the governor on 25 October. It was signed Belle Elmore Crippen. Part of it read: 'I don't want to be responsible for your demise if I can save you in this way but I will never come forward personally, as I am happy now.' The programme stated that the second letter, dated 22 October and received several days after the first, was passed on to his superiors by the prison governor, who was anxious to find out about its authenticity. The reply came that it had gone to the Home Secretary. The programme stated that 'the Home Secretary, Winston Churchill . . . slipped it into his pocket and plainly forgot about it because it was certainly never given to the defence as it should have been'. The documentary also revealed that 'Newly discovered papers show that they [Crippen's defence team] weren't told of a further discovery. At the same time that Cora tried to remove £600 from their deposit account, she had hired a removal firm to take six trunks away from Hilldrop Crescent to the home of an American music teacher in Bayswater.' The investigation also included some convincing evidence of possible contamination of the remains, which might have resulted in inaccurate assumptions being made at the time. Ten slides of the remains, used for scientific analysis in 1910, still exist and were examined by present-day experts. Some doubt as to the findings offered in evidence in 1910 was expressed.

Notwithstanding the doubts that have been raised over the years about Crippen's guilt, the fact that human remains were found in the cellar at 39 Hilldrop Crescent has never been in doubt. This notorious case will attract repeated investigation and re-examination for years to come.

6

Murder by Arsenical Poisoning?

THE KILLING OF ELIZA BARROW

Finsbury Park, 1911

Lancashire-born Frederick Henry Seddon was employed as District Superintendent of Canvassers for North London with the London & Manchester
Industrial Assurance Company, a position he had occupied since 1901. A
freemason and one-time chapel-goer and preacher, Seddon had learned the
value of money early in life. He was hard-working, thrifty and eager to save.
He was willing to turn his hand to any type of business where money could be
made and took pride in attending to even the simplest of transactions in
meticulous detail. However, Seddon was not a particularly likeable man. His
general manner and air of superiority tended to alienate him from those he
came into contact with. His lack of affability went strongly against him when
he went on trial for murder, and this is evident in the trial transcript.

In 1909, when this particular account begins, in addition to his insurance
work Seddon owned a second-hand clothes business which he ran in his wife's
name at 276 Seven Sisters Road, Finsbury Park, and he and his family lived
above the shop. Seddon invested his additional income in mortgaged property
and regularly sold it on at a profit. After one successful business deal he
bought a fourteen-roomed house at 63 Tollington Park, situated north of
Seven Sisters Road between Stroud Green Road and Hornsey Road, in the
area of North London that lies between Holloway and Finsbury Park. It was
originally purchased as an investment to turn into flats, but Seddon was quick
to realise that this house could provide a home for himself and his family, as
well as a basement office, and there would still be room for tenants in the four
rooms on the top floor.

In November 1909 the family moved in. Seddon's insurance company employers found him scrupulously honest and so exact in his accounting that they allowed him to bank their money in his own account, and were pleased to give him 5s a week rent for his basement room office in which he administered their business. For the convenience of business callers to the house the basement could be reached by an outside flight of steps. An inside flight led to other parts of the house.

Towards the end of the year Mr and Mrs Seddon fell out and briefly separated, but their differences were soon mended and Margaret Seddon found herself pregnant again with her fifth child. Then on 20 June 1910 Seddon instructed the house agents to obtain a tenant for his top-floor flat, for which he would receive a rental income of 12s 6d a week. The two other floors and the basement were occupied by the Seddon household – Mr and Mrs Seddon, Mr Seddon's 73-year-old father William Seddon, four children (with a fifth to follow) and an eccentric servant named Mary Chater, a former mental nurse who was somewhat unhinged herself. The Seddons also employed a charwoman, Mrs Rutt, although she lived elsewhere. As well as the rental income he received from his company and the flat, Seddon also charged his two sons 6s a week for living at home.

Eliza Barrow was a 49-year-old spinster of independent means with private property amounting to about £4,000, which included the Buck's Head and adjacent barber's shop in Camden Town. She had taken on the responsibility for looking after two orphaned children of a former landlady in Clapton. An adolescent girl called Hilda was away at boarding school, but 8-year-old Ernie Grant lived with Miss Barrow in a succession of lodgings. In about May 1909 they went to lodge with

Frederick H. Seddon. *(Author's collection)*

Miss Eliza Barrow, the victim. *(Author's collection)*

No. 63 Tollington Park; Seddon's office in the basement could be reached by going down the stairs to the right of the front steps. Miss Barrow and little Ernie Grant occupied the top floor. *(Paul T. Langley Welch)*

Miss Barrow's cousins, Mr and Mrs Frank Vonderahe at 31 Evershot Road, a turning off Tollington Park. However, the Vonderahes and Miss Barrow did not get on and Miss Barrow once spat at Mrs Vonderahe. Miss Barrow decided to look for lodgings with her friends Mr and Mrs Robert Hook and they all moved into 63 Tollington Park. Mr Hook was an engine-driver and he and his wife were to lodge with Miss Barrow in exchange for Mrs Hook's domestic services.

By 1 August 1910 twelve people were living in Seddon's house. It was not long before Miss Barrow found fault with the Hooks. Miss Barrow was not a very likeable person and most people found her difficult to get on with, as became clear from evidence given by various witnesses during the trial. Seddon became aware of the lack of harmony on the top floor and decided that Miss Barrow and the Hooks were not suitable tenants. He informed Miss Barrow that they would have to leave. However, when Miss Barrow turned to Mr Seddon for help she convinced him that it was the Hooks who were at fault. He was persuaded and the Hooks were asked to leave. They did so very quickly after Seddon posted a notice to quit on their door, leaving Miss Barrow and little Ernie Grant as the only occupants of the top floor.

Frederick Seddon found a soulmate in Miss Barrow. Like him, Eliza Barrow had a fondness for money and investments. She stood about 5ft 4in tall and was rather plump. During the trial evidence was given that she dressed badly, was parsimonious in her habits and had been prone to alcoholic indulgence. She paid 12*s* 6*d* a week in rent for her rooms and, following the departure of the Hooks, 7*s* a week to the Seddons' daughter Maggie for cooking and cleaning.

Following Lloyd George's famous budget of 1909, like many other ladies of her class in similar circumstances Miss Barrow had become increasingly concerned that his 'soak the rich' policy would reduce her to penury. At the trial Seddon said of her: 'It was her property that was worrying her. She said she had a public house at Camden Town called the Buck's Head, and it was the principal source of her income; she had a lot of trouble with the ground landlords, and she said that Lloyd George's Budget had upset licensed premises by increased taxation.' Seddon gave Miss Barrow reassurance and offered her financial advice. This culminated in their coming to a financial arrangement that would benefit both parties. In exchange for an annuity amounting to £52, Seddon took from Miss Barrow a seventeen-year lease on the Buck's Head and the adjacent 1 Buck Street, a small building then occupied by a barber's shop. On 14 October 1910 Miss Barrow transferred ownership of her India Stock, valued at £1,600, to Seddon. He agreed to pay her a lifetime annuity amounting to £103 4s, in addition to the £52 to which he had already committed. Seddon sold the India Stock for £1,520 and invested the money in fourteen tenement houses in the East End, at Coutts Road, Stepney, for a rental income of £200 a year. Seddon paid Miss Barrow her annuity in regular instalments and she was delighted, because the money she received as a result of Seddon's financial advice exceeded the amount she had been receiving in dividends.

London sweltered in a heatwave during the last week of August and the first week of September 1911. On the morning of Friday 1 September Miss Barrow was taken ill with what was diagnosed by Dr Sworn as epidemic diarrhoea. He prescribed bismuth and morphia. He said she was very ill and added that her mental state appeared as bad as her physical health. He returned on the Saturday and on the Sunday, but there was no improvement. Miss Barrow found it difficult to take her medication, so he gave her an effervescing mixture of citrate of potash and bicarbonate of soda. He could give her nothing for the diarrhoea, which was very severe. Dr Sworn stated at the trial, when asked if there was an epidemic of flies at the time: 'I have never seen so many as I saw in that room. I put it down to the smell of the motions which would attract them.' The doctor suggested that she should go to hospital, but Miss Barrow refused. She also refused to have a nurse, saying that Mrs Seddon 'could attend to her very well indeed and she was very attentive'.

On Monday 4 September Mrs Seddon said that Miss Barrow instructed her to go and get some flypapers. She did not want the sticky type but those that you wet. On Tuesday Miss Barrow was a little better and she called for Ernie Grant to sleep with her, which was her habit. (Little Ernie referred to Miss Barrow as 'Chickie'.) For the next three days Dr Sworn continued prescribing the effervescing medicine but on the 9th he gave Miss Barrow an additional blue pill containing mercury, as 'her motion was so offensive'. The stench emanating from Miss Barrow's room permeated the entire house. It became so bad that carbolic sheets were hung in the rooms in an attempt to fumigate the air.

Miss Barrow began to grow worried about what would happen to little Ernie and Hilda if she were to die. She asked Seddon to draw up a will for her. He did so and the will was witnessed by his married sister, Emily Longley, who was visiting at the time, and Mrs Seddon. The will made Frederick H. Seddon sole executor, 'to hold all my personal belongings, furniture, clothing and jewellery in trust' until Ernest and Hilda Grant came of age. Miss Eliza Barrow died at about 6.15 a.m. on Thursday 14 September 1911. Seddon went to Dr Sworn's house and told him the news. The doctor made out a death certificate giving the cause of death as 'epidemic diarrhoea'.

William Nodes, undertaker, operated from 201 Holloway Road and had a branch office at 78 Stroud Green Road, a short distance from Seddon's house. Seddon called on Mr Nodes at about 11.30 a.m. on 14 September to arrange Miss Barrow's funeral. The funeral took place two days later. When giving evidence at the trial, Mr Nodes was asked questions regarding the funeral arrangements and what some might consider the unseemly haste in which Miss Barrow was buried. Mr Nodes stated:

> If we did not bury on Saturday it would mean burying on Monday, and having regard to the state that the body was in and the diarrhoea that had taken place, the warmth of the weather, and the fact that there was no lead lining to the coffin, it seemed quite reasonable that the body should be buried on Saturday. . . . I explained to him what kind of funeral it would be for the price; it was a £4 funeral really, and it would mean a coffin, polished and ornamented with handles and inside lining, a composite carriage, the necessary bearers, and the fees at Islington Cemetery, and it included the interment in the grave at Finchley. I do not know that I specified what kind of grave she would be buried in, but it would mean interment in a public grave, a grave dug by the cemetery people, who allow interments in it at a certain price, which included the use of the clergyman. By a 'public grave' I mean a grave which is not the particular property of any individual; it is used for more than one person. I think it was distinctly understood by Mr Seddon that it would not be a private grave.

Seddon was quick to point out that Miss Barrow was not a relation of his and, in consideration of the business he had brought him, accepted 12s 6d commission from William Nodes. The funeral took place on Saturday afternoon; Mr and Mrs F.H. Seddon and William Seddon travelled in the composite carriage to the cemetery in East Finchley.

On 20 September Frank Vonderahe heard that his cousin had been ill and called to see her. He was amazed when the Seddons' maid told him that she had died and that the funeral had already taken place. The Vonderahes called

Stroud Green Road as it looked in the early years of the twentieth century. Tollington Park is a turning off Stroud Green Road to the right; No. 78, the premises of William Nodes, undertaker, was towards the end of the buildings on the right. *(John D. Murray)*

again to see Mr Seddon, who told them he had written to them in Evershot Street telling them about the death and showed them a copy of his letter. The Vonderahes said they had moved to Corbyn Street, but letters were forwarded to them and they had never received it. Seddon's copy of the letter was later produced as evidence in court:

63 Tollington Park, London, N
14th Septr., 1911.
Mr. Frank E. Vonderahe.

Dear Sir, – I sincerely regret to have to inform you of the death of your Cousin, Miss Eliza Mary Barrow, at 6 a.m. this morning, from epidemic diarrhoea. The funeral will take place on Saturday next about 1 to 2 p.m.

Please inform Albert Edward and Emma Marion Vonderahe of her decease, and let me know if you or they wish to attend the funeral.

I must also inform you that she made a 'will' on the 11th instant leaving what she died possessed of to Hilda and Ernest Grant, and appointed myself as sole executor under the 'will' – yours respectfully, F. H. Seddon

Mr. Frank Ernest Vonderahe,
31, Evershot Road,
Finsbury Park, N.

The Vonderahes admitted that they had no particular liking for Miss Barrow, but they expressed astonishment that she had not been buried in the family vault in Highgate Cemetery. Seddon said that he believed that it was full, but the Vonderahes contradicted him. Seddon told them that it would be an easy matter if the family wished to have Miss Barrow's body moved to Highgate. The Vonderahes did not want to pursue the point, but they were anxious to know what had happened to Eliza Barrow's money. Robert Hook later testified that Miss Barrow had £420 4s 3d, mostly in gold coin, when he helped her count it in 1906, and the money was kept in fifteen bags in a cash-box. The Vonderahes also knew that Miss Barrow had a considerable sum of cash. When Seddon told them there wasn't any, they weren't satisfied. They created a fuss and became highly suspicious about the circumstances surrounding their cousin's death. They continued to pester and accuse, and eventually decided to report their suspicions to the police, who began an investigation.

Miss Barrow's body was exhumed on 15 November and examined by pathologist Dr Bernard Spilsbury, in the presence of Dr Willcox, at Finchley Mortuary. The body was in a remarkable state of preservation. Virtually no decomposition had taken place, although, as is usual, the body had lost a considerable amount of its water content. Traces of arsenic were found in the remains. An inquest was held on 23 November at which both Mr and Mrs Seddon gave evidence. In his report to the coroner's court Dr Spilsbury stated,

> I found no disease in any of the organs sufficient to account for death, except in the stomach and intestines. In the intestines I found a little reddening of the inner surface of the upper part. . . . The body was remarkably well preserved, both externally and internally. This would suggest that death was due to some poison having a preservative effect, or to the presence of some preserving agent. I think the arsenic that Dr Willcox says he found would account for the preservation of the body. . . . The reddening . . . was evidence of inflammation. I don't think there is anything to distinguish this from natural gastro-enteritis.

Dr Willcox stated that in his opinion there must have been more than two grains of arsenic present in the body at the time of death; that the death was due to acute arsenical poisoning; and that Miss Barrow must have taken a moderately large fatal dose less than three, and probably less than two, days before her death. The inquest was adjourned.

On 29 November Dr Willcox made a further examination of Miss Barrow's remains and found arsenic present in all the organs and other parts tested. Neither the family nor the authorities transferred Miss Barrow's body to Highgate Cemetery, made possible by her exhumation. In due course it was returned to another grave in the cemetery at East Finchley.

At 7 p.m. on 4 December Seddon was arrested outside his home. According to the police, when he was told he would be arrested for the wilful murder of Miss Eliza Barrow and for administering poison, Seddon replied, 'Absurd. What a terrible charge – wilful murder. It is the first of [sic] our family that has ever been charged with such a crime.' At the time of his arrest, in addition to 63 Tollington Park, Seddon owned seventeen other properties.

The inquest was resumed on 14 December. Frederick Seddon attended in custody and reserved his evidence for the trial that was to follow. The jury returned their verdict as follows:

> That the said Eliza Mary Barrow died on the 14th of September, 1911, of arsenical poisoning at 63, Tollington Park, the arsenic having been administered to her by some person or persons unknown. And so the jurors aforesaid do further say that the said person or persons unknown on the 13th or 14th or 13th and 14th days of September, 1911, did feloniously, wilfully, and of malice aforethought murder and slay against the peace of our Lord the King, his Crown and Dignity, the said Eliza Mary Barrow.

During the weeks that followed Eliza Barrow's death Mrs Seddon had exchanged thirty-three £5 notes in local shops. Their serial numbers showed them to have been Miss Barrow's. Mrs Seddon never gave a satisfactory explanation for having endorsed them as 'Mrs Scott' of 10 or 18 Evershot Street. She was arrested on 15 January 1912.

The trial of 40-year-old Frederick H. Seddon and 38-year-old Margaret Anne Seddon at the Central Criminal Court in the Sessions House, Old Bailey, opened on 4 March 1912 before Mr Justice Bucknill. Counsel for the Crown was led by the Attorney-General, the Right Honourable Sir Rufus D. Isaacs KC, MP, R.D. Muir, S.A.T. Rowlatt and Travers Humphreys. Counsel for Frederick Seddon were Edward Marshall Hall KC, MP, Mr Dunstan and Mr Orr; and for Margaret Seddon, Gervais Rentoul. The trial lasted ten days.

The weight of evidence assembled against the Seddons centred on the amount of arsenic found in Miss Barrow's remains and the acquisition of flypapers containing arsenic. Flypapers had been purchased at Thorley's Chemists at 27 Crouch Hill. Walter Thorley knew Seddon's daughter because she was friendly with his own daughter. He testified that on 26 August 1911 Margaret Seddon (Maggie) bought a threepenny packet of Mather's flypapers. There were six in a packet and the label on the outside proclaimed: 'To poison flies, wasps, ants, mosquitoes, &c. Prepared only by the sole proprietors, W. Mather Limited, Dyer Street, Manchester. Poison. These arsenic fly-papers can only be sold by registered chemists, and in accordance with the provisions of the Pharmacy Act.' The directions for use stated:

The Seddons in the dock at the Old Bailey. *(Author's collection)*

'Spread each paper on a dish or plate and keep moist with cold water. A little sugar, beer or wine added two or three times a day makes them more attractive. Caution. Remove the tray or dish beyond the reach of children and out of the way of domestic animals.'

It was shown that if boiled, one flypaper could produce 5 grains of arsenic, 2 grains being a fatal dose: 2.1 grains were found in Miss Barrow's remains. Various theories were put forward as to how arsenic might have got into Miss Barrow's body. It was suggested that she might have taken it herself in small quantities over a long period, a practice considered beneficial in some quarters. Mr Marshall Hall was not convinced that the tests made on Miss Barrow's body gave an accurate reading of the amount of arsenic the body contained, due to the body having shrunk as a result of water loss. Regarding the famous Marsh Test conducted by Dr Willcox and used to establish the amount of arsenic contained in the body, Mr Marshall Hall said: 'It is theory, that is all. It is scientific theory of the highest possible character, but he cannot prove it to me by ocular demonstration, and it is not the sort of theory upon which a man's life ought to be put in peril.' Regarding the 2.1 grains of arsenic found in Miss Barrow's body tissue, he said,

> Dr Willcox admits that that is purely a matter of calculation. You cannot get at that for this reason, that you cannot get at the weight of the muscle tissue, and therefore you have to estimate it. It has never been estimated on a dead body, and therefore you have to deal with it with a *live* body, and with a live body it is calculated that the muscle tissue accounts for 44 per cent – three-fifths [*sic*] of the total weight of the body; that is the total weight of the live body. This body had shrunk from something like 10 stones to under 5 stones, so that there was a wastage of half.

Mr Marshall Hall continued to protest that the calculations made concerning the quantity of arsenic in the body had not been accurately

William Seddon (Frederick Seddon's father), Elizabeth Chater (the Seddons' maid), Mrs Rutt, Maggie Seddon (the couple's eldest daughter) and Margaret A. Seddon. (*Author's collection*)

Sir Rufus Isaacs KCVO, KC, MP, Attorney-General from 1910 to 1913. *(Author's collection)*

calculated and therefore did not present the true facts. He concluded this point by adding,

> What I say is this, and what I ask you to find as a fact in this case is this, that there is arsenic in this body, that it did not cause the death, that she died of gastro-enteritis – that is, that she died of epidemic diarrhoea. Possibly the condition may have been aggravated, but that there is no evidence in the body was of itself sufficient to cause death [*sic*], because you cannot rely scientifically on the quantity alleged to have been found.

Despite Mr Marshall Hall's magnificent defence, Seddon's own performance in the witness box went against him. He was simply not a likeable man. The often flippant or glib answers Seddon gave under cross-examination did not endear him to the jury. The Attorney-General, Sir Rufus D. Isaacs, asked Seddon: 'Miss Barrow lived with you from 26th July 1910, till the morning of 14th September, 1911?' Seddon replied, 'Yes.' Sir Rufus then asked 'Did you like her?' Seddon replied with a question: 'Did I like her?' Sir Rufus then said, 'Yes, that is the question.' Seddon replied, 'She was not a woman that you could be in love with, but I deeply sympathised with her.' Later Sir Rufus said, 'I should like you to understand, if the ordinary expectation of her life was twenty-one years – the life of a woman of that age – and you thought, as you told us, it was going to be less than that, what sort of view did you form in your own mind about it?' Seddon replied, 'I could not say; I could not tell how long the woman was going to live.' Sir Rufus asked, 'But some years less?' To which Seddon replied, 'I have known people in consumption outlive healthy people; as the old saying is, "A creaky gate hangs a long time".'

Much of the evidence assembled against the Seddons was circumstantial. However, it was Mrs Seddon who had continuous access to the sickroom and it was she who is known to have endorsed £165 in £5 notes using a false name following Miss Barrow's death (at today's values about £8,250). That Frederick Seddon had expressed his willingness to look after little Ernie following Miss Barrow's demise and to take over caring for Hilda, before his arrest, must indicate that despite his own miserly ways, the man did possess some degree of humanity – little Ernie Grant said that unlike the Vonderahes, Chickie and the Seddons were always nice to him. As Filson Young, compiler of the Seddon volume in the *Notable British Trials* series, eloquently put it, Seddon was convicted not because the Crown succeeded in proving his guilt, but because he failed to prove his innocence.

The trial ended with Seddon found guilty of the wilful murder of Eliza Mary Barrow and sentenced to death. Mrs Seddon was acquitted. Before sentence of death was pronounced Seddon gave a long and powerful speech, quoting facts and figures, and gave a full protestation of his innocence. His lengthy address ended,

> You have also referred, my lord, to the letter that I sent to the Vonderahes after her death wherein I omit to state anything at all regarding the money. I thought I pointed out in the witness-box that at that moment when I wrote that letter, the search having been made in the box, there was no money to mention. I had not had the money. The prosecution has never traced the money to me. The prosecution has not traced anything to me in the shape of money, which is the greatest motive suggested by the prosecution in this case for my committing the diabolical crime of which I declare before the Great Architect of the Universe I am not guilty, my lord. Anything more I might have to say I do not suppose will be of any account, but, still, if it is the last words that I speak, I am not guilty of the crime for which I stand committed.

Seddon concluded his speech by raising his hands as if he was taking a freemason's oath. The judge, too, was a freemason. He was moved to tears. An appeal was heard on 1 April 1912 and dismissed the following day. There was an enormous public outcry against the verdict and a petition containing over 250,000 signatures claiming Seddon's innocence. Despite this overwhelming public support it was decided that the law must take its course.

Seddon remained interested in money to the end. On the day before his execution he called for his solicitor to ascertain what certain articles of his furniture had fetched when sold at auction. He was concerned that everything possible should be salvaged from the ruins of his fortune in order to safeguard the future of his wife and children. When told of the relatively small sum of money the sale had realised, Seddon struck the table and said scornfully,

'That's done it!' He displayed no emotion regarding his own impending fate. An unprecedented crowd of over 7,000 people gathered outside Pentonville Prison on the day of his execution, 18 April 1912. John Ellis was the executioner.

It seems incredible that Seddon, a man of fastidious habits and meticulous attention to detail, having supposedly poisoned his victim could make such an elementary mistake in allowing the principal evidence for the crime to remain available for scrutiny by the authorities, that evidence being the body of Miss Eliza Barrow. In Seddon's defence, Mr Marshall Hall pointed out that there was no evidence to prove to the contrary that Miss Barrow, ill with diarrhoea and extremely thirsty, had not accidentally drunk the water in which the flypapers had been soaked and which stood in the saucer near the bed. As Mr Marshall Hall pointed out, 'Why did not Seddon, were he guilty of poisoning Miss Barrow, have the body cremated?' Why not indeed? And if Miss Barrow were indeed murdered, it seems the evidence points to Mrs Seddon as the culprit.

7

The Brides in the Bath Murderer

GEORGE JOSEPH SMITH

Holloway, 1914

On 18 December 1914 a newly married young woman died in Bismarck Road, Upper Holloway, situated off Highgate Hill, to the north of the City of London (and close to the spot where the celebrated Dick Whittington is said to have turned again). The tragic death excited sufficient attention to warrant its inclusion in the *News of the World* following the inquest, which was held on 1 January 1915. The article brought about the downfall of one of the most infamous wife-killers of all time, George Joseph Smith, the harmonium-playing petty criminal, confidence trickster, antique dealer and serial bigamist known as the Brides in the Bath murderer.

George Joseph Smith was born on 11 January 1872 at 92 Roman Road, Bethnal Green, in the East End. At the age of 9 he was sentenced to eight years in a reformatory at Gravesend. It may have been during his incarceration there that he developed a total contempt for the law; his subsequent conduct would certainly seem to bear that out. After his release at the age of 16 it was not long before Smith found himself in trouble with the law again. On 7 February 1891 he was sentenced at Lambeth Police Court to six months' hard labour. His crime was stealing a bicycle. Not long after his release from this sentence he spent three years in the Northamptonshire Regiment, but he then lapsed into his old ways, which resulted in yet another twelve months' hard labour in 1896, when he was sentenced at the North London Sessions for larceny and receiving stolen goods. However, this time he used an alias when he was charged – George Baker, the first of his many false names. In fact it was one of his numerous lady-friends who had actually done the stealing for him.

George Joseph Smith. *(Stewart P. Evans)*

Smith had an eye for the ladies and judging by his success in the marital stakes, it would seem the ladies had an eye for him too. It is difficult to imagine from the photographs that exist of this infamous rogue what the attraction was. Clearly Smith possessed sufficient charm and *savoir-faire* to make him irresistible. One of his 'brides', in fact his first bigamous bride, whom he married in 1899 and who survived, described him thus: 'He had an extraordinary power. . . . This power lay in his eyes. . . . When he looked at you, you had the feeling that you were being magnetised. They were little eyes that seemed to rob you of your will.' (This first bigamous wife is not identifiable by name. Possibly at some point in the investigations into Smith's background, perhaps at her request, her identity was concealed.) Smith may well have possessed the necessary charms to attract numerous females, but he certainly adopted a parsimonious lifestyle once he had made his conquest. He travelled third class, lodged his brides cheaply and took them by bicycle or on foot to places of free public entertainment.

On his release from prison in 1897 he went to Leicester, where he opened a baker's shop at 28 Russell Square. The money he used for this, £115, was stolen for him from her employers by his lady-friend, who had provided such services for Smith before. This time Smith called himself George Oliver Love. It was during his time in Leicester that Smith met Caroline Beatrice Thornhill, an 18-year-old maidservant. Her father was a bootmaker. He strongly disapproved of the 26-year-old suitor who presented himself as his daughter's future husband, but Caroline married her suitor on 17 January 1898 and became Mrs Love. Some years later she described her husband as having, 'Complexion fair, hair brown, ginger moustache, peak chin, on left arm a very large scar, military walk, stands 5ft 9ins.' She also said that during the time she knew him she never saw him do any work. Within six months the bakery business failed. Smith treated his new wife unkindly and often vented his frustration by beating her. Distraught and fearful of her husband she left and fled to Nottingham. Smith soon followed her, made amends and once again won her over.

Smith used his charms to persuade Caroline that they could make a success of their marriage and an easy profit into the bargain. His gullible young wife was taken in and Smith devised a plan. He and Mrs Love moved first to London, where he posed as her employer and gave references to secure her work with various families for whom she was engaged as a maid. She stole from them. Similar scams were perpetrated in Brighton, Hove and Hastings. In the autumn of 1899, while trying to sell some silver spoons she had stolen, Mrs Love was arrested in Hastings. She was given a 12-month prison sentence; her husband had conveniently disappeared.

Smith's callous abandonment of his wife deeply hurt and angered her. He used the year of his wife's absence to cement a relationship with a middle-aged boarding-house keeper, whom he bigamously married in London and then quickly relieved her of her money before leaving her for pastures new. On her release from prison Mrs Love sought her revenge. She found her husband and successfully incriminated him. On 9 January 1901 Smith was jailed at Hastings for two years for receiving stolen goods. After his release from prison in 1903 he went to Leicester in search of Caroline, but, fortunately for her, this time Mrs Love had made good her escape by emigrating to Canada, and Smith did not follow her.

Smith then embarked upon wooing an assortment of ladies of means, many of whom succumbed to his charms, some to his bigamous marital bed and three of his six known bigamous wives to a watery death. The full extent of Smith's amorous adventures will never be known. The assortment of one-time besotted and later humiliated ladies, too embarrassed to come forward, may have amounted to a considerable number. The years where little is known about his activities may hold many a sad story and his exploits before 1903 and after 1908 would seem to bear this out.

It was in June 1908 that he met a widow called Florence Wilson. They had a whirlwind courtship lasting three weeks and then married in London. Shortly after the wedding Smith persuaded his Florence to withdraw £30 from her post office savings account, which she gave to him. He then took her to the Franco-British Exhibition at White City on 3 July. Having left her sitting comfortably on a bench while he went to get a newspaper, he hurried to their lodgings in Camden, packed her belongings and absconded. Having sold her possessions, he used the money to set himself up in business as a second-hand dealer in Gloucester Road, Bristol. (At this point it is worth mentioning that the £115 he used to set up his bakery business up in 1897 represented about two years' wages for an average, comfortably well-off working man at that time. Mrs Wilson's £30 was worth more than six months' wages.) This move to Bristol brought Smith into contact with a woman to whom he would remain attached for the rest of his life.

In Bristol Smith advertised for a housekeeper and engaged Edith Mabel Pegler. Romance followed and he married her on 30 July 1908, using his own name. Edith may well have been the one true love of his life for he did not rob, desert or murder her, and returned to her many times with the proceeds of his subsequent 'marriages'. Their business as antiques dealers saw them travelling to Bedford, Luton, Croydon, London and Southend-on-Sea. Smith often went away on business alone and Edith accepted her 'husband's' often extended trips without question. He would communicate with her by letter or postcard and would occasionally send her money. If she ran out of funds during a particularly long absence, Edith would return to her mother in Bristol. Smith would attribute the sometimes substantial sums he brought home to her to successful business deals. When he told her he had been abroad to Canada or Spain, she believed him entirely.

In October 1909 Smith married his next bride. Calling himself George Rose, he met a spinster clerk named Sarah Freeman in Southampton. He charmed her and convinced her he was a man of means supported by a wealthy aunt. He usually dressed well and his appearance in a frock coat and top hat gave the impression that he was well off. The newly married Mr and Mrs Rose moved to lodgings in London. His latest bride was very keen to help her husband achieve his ambition of having an antiques business and to that end Sarah withdrew her savings, some £260, and also sold some government stock. Once he had obtained her money, she was surplus to requirements. On 5 November Smith took Sarah out for the day; they visited the National Gallery. While Smith went to the lavatory, his wife waited patiently for him. He never returned. While she waited Smith went back to their lodgings in Clapham, removed her belongings and sold them. Sarah was left with three empty tea chests and a bicycle, totally destitute. In all he had obtained around £400 from her, about four years' wages for the average working man. With the money he brought Edith to Southend, where he established a second-hand furniture shop at 22 Glenmore Street, purchased for £270. He also took out a £30 mortgage on the property and bought a house at 86 Ashley Down Road, Bristol, largely on loan.

In 1910 Beatrice (Bessie) Constance Mundy, then living in a boarding house in Clifton, a fashionable Bristol suburb, was a 31-year-old spinster. Her father, who died in 1904, had been a bank manager at Warminster in Wiltshire and had left his daughter a small fortune held in trust, so the capital could not be touched. It amounted to over £2,500 in gilt-edged securities, administered by a family trust headed by her uncle. Bessie received a monthly allowance of about £8 – a lesser amount than funds allowed, but her uncle had a low opinion of her ability to handle money. As a result the trust fund accumulated.

While out walking one day Miss Mundy had a chance meeting with a picture restorer by the name of Henry Williams, otherwise known as George Joseph Smith. Within just a few days Smith had swept Bessie off her feet and they were soon on their way to Weymouth, where they moved into lodgings at 14 Rodwell Avenue. Bessie and Smith were married at Weymouth Registry Office on 26 August 1910, whereupon Bessie wrote:

Dear Uncle,

I got married today, my husband is writing tonight.
    Yours truly,

     B.Williams.

Bessie Mundy.
(Stewart P. Evans)

Bessie's husband wrote to her uncle:

> Bessie hopes you will forward as much money as possible at your earliest by registered letter. Am pleased to say Bessie is in perfect health, and we are both looking forward to a bright and happy future. Believe me, yours faithfully, Henry Williams.

By the time Smith had got his hands on the accumulated balance in Bessie's trust fund, which amounted to £138, it was 13 December. Having cajoled the money out of her he promptly left Bessie, but not before writing a letter giving her instructions on how to conceal her shame and accusing her of having given him venereal disease:

> Dearest,
> I fear you have blighted all my bright hopes of a happy future. I have caught from you a disease which is called the bad disorder. For you to be in such a state proves you could not have kept yourself morally clean. . . . For the sake of my health and honour, and yours too, I must go to London . . . to get properly cured of this disease. It will cost me a great deal of money, because it might take years. . . . Tell the landlady and everyone else that I have gone to France. But tell your uncle the truth. . . . If he happens to ask you about the money which was sent to you in a yellow bag, say two days after I had gone you happened to go on the beach and fall asleep and when you woke the bag of money was gone. . . . Whatever you do, stick to everything you say. Never alter it or else you will get mixed up and make a fool of yourself.

Having achieved his aim of getting hold of some ready cash, Smith did not go to London but returned to Edith, who was in Bristol. Bessie left Weymouth and went to live with a friend, Mrs Sarah Tuckett, in Weston-super-Mare, much nearer to her former home in Clifton. One morning during March 1912 Bessie went out at about 11 o'clock and during her stroll along the esplanade spotted her husband, Henry Williams. She approached him, but instead of reprimanding him or reporting him to the authorities for having absconded with her money, she once again succumbed to his charms. He told her he had been looking for her for over a year. Mrs Tuckett said that Bessie returned at about 1 o'clock. 'She was very excited.' Smith called at Bessie's lodgings at about 3 o'clock. Mrs Tuckett took an instant dislike to Smith, but Bessie told her that she had forgiven her husband and had decided to go back to him and they had already consulted a solicitor. Mrs Tuckett told Smith that it was her duty to wire Bessie's aunt to come at once. However, Bessie left that afternoon with Smith and promised to return in the evening. She did not take her belongings. Mrs Tuckett never saw her again.

Bessie and Smith went from town to town while he made enquiries as to how he might legally take possession of her fortune. In May the couple rented a property at 80 High Street, Herne Bay, where Smith set up a brass plate proclaiming that he was an antiques dealer. By then he had discovered that if Bessie made a will in her husband's favour, in the event of her death he would inherit her fortune. Bessie's fate was sealed. On Monday 8 July separate wills were drawn up, each in the other's favour. On the 9th the couple bought a second-hand zinc bath and Bessie herself beat down the price from £2 to £1 17s 6d. This was the bath in which she was to die.

Smith then set about convincing Bessie that she was not well. (This was a technique he would also use on his later 'brides'.) On Wednesday 10 July Smith took Bessie to visit the recently qualified Dr French. He told the doctor that his wife had suffered a fit. However, all Bessie complained of was a headache. At 1.30 a.m. on Friday 12 July Dr French was called to 80 High Street because Mrs Williams had suffered another fit. He could find nothing particularly wrong with her. It was a warm night and Mrs Williams was in bed, looking as if she had just woken up. The doctor prescribed a sedative. The next afternoon Dr French saw the Williamses taking a walk and all appeared to be well. On the same day Bessie wrote to her uncle at the suggestion of her husband and she told him about the fits.

On the morning of Saturday 13 July, at a little after 7 a.m., Bessie prepared to have a bath in one of the upstairs spare rooms, and made numerous journeys carrying buckets of water from the kitchen. Her husband went out to buy some fish. Bessie, with her hair in curling pins, got into the bath. Some time afterwards her husband returned. At about 8 o'clock, Dr French received a note from Mr Williams: 'Can you come at once? I'm afraid my wife is dead!'

On his arrival at 80 High Street Dr French discovered the body of Mrs Williams in her bath in an upstairs room. The body was naked and partially submerged, her legs were resting out of the water on the end of the bath and in her right hand she was clutching a bar of soap. Dr French informed the police of the fatality and later that morning PC Kitchingham took a statement from the widower. Bessie's body had been laid on the floor near the bath in which she had died and during the afternoon a woman came to lay her out.

Smith sent a wire to Bessie's uncle: 'Bessie died in fit this morning. Letter following.' Smith then wrote a letter explaining how shocked he was at the loss of his dear wife and gave an account of the circumstances of her death in the bath. No post-mortem examination was carried out on Bessie Mundy's body. An inquest was held on Monday 15 July and the bereaved husband wept throughout. Dr French stated that in his opinion the woman drowned as a result of a fit of epilepsy in the bath. The jury returned a verdict of misadventure, 'the cause of death being that while taking a bath she had an epileptic seizure causing her to fall back into the water and be drowned'.

At 2.30 p.m. on Tuesday 16 July Bessie was buried in a common grave. Smith had arranged the funeral before any of her relatives had the chance to make arrangements to attend. Smith never paid for the bath in which Bessie Mundy died. Having obtained credit, he returned it to the ironmonger's six days later. It had served its purpose and was of no further use to him.

Bessie Mundy's estate was proved at £2,571 and as Smith had arranged, under the terms of her will her 'husband' inherited it all. Despite her relatives' attempts to contest the will, Bessie's money had been paid to her sole executor and legatee, Henry Williams. Smith opened several bank accounts and used some of the money to purchase seven houses in Bristol and an annuity that brought him £76 a year. While all Bessie's affairs were being wound up, Smith remained active elsewhere. During the month after Bessie Mundy's death, August 1912, Smith contacted Edith Pegler and told her to join him in Margate. Before he disappeared again in 1913, Smith and Edith moved first to Tunbridge Wells, then to Bristol, Weston-super-Mare and finally back to Bristol. (Edith's account of her relationship with Smith indicated that it was not an unhappy one, although she stated that he did beat her from time to time.)

In October 1913 Smith was once again on the coast, at Southsea in Hampshire. He was, as usual, on the prowl for a new bride. Alice Burnham was a buxom, 25-year-old private nurse who looked after an elderly male invalid. Smith spotted her praying in a Wesleyan chapel. Romance quickly followed and Smith married her at Portsmouth registry office on 4 November – but not before discovering that she was not without means and that her father, a fruit grower from Buckinghamshire, was looking after £104 for her. Miss Burnham's father Charles met Smith before the marriage took place and took a thorough dislike to him. At this marriage ceremony Smith once again used his real name.

He wrote to Alice's father suggesting that her money should be handed over, but her father was anxious to know more about his new son-in-law's background and proceeded to investigate. When Smith heard about this by letter he replied to his father-in-law's with a postcard, which was read out at the trial:

> Sir,
> In answer to your application regarding my parentage, my mother was a bus-horse, my father a cab-driver, my sister a roughrider over the Arctic regions. My brothers were all gallant sailors on a steam-roller. This is the only information I can give to those who are not entitled to ask such questions contained in the letter I received on the 24th inst.
>
> Your despised son-in-law
> G. SMITH

Smith got Alice's £104 from her reluctant father after he engaged the services of a solicitor. He also persuaded her to withdraw £27 9s 5d from her savings bank. He had already taken out a life insurance policy on his wife's life for £500 on 3 November, the day before the marriage took place. Alice made out a will in her husband's favour and Smith decided to take his new bride on an out-of-season holiday to the Lancashire resort of Blackpool. They arrived there on 10 December. First they visited a boarding house in Adelaide Street,

Alice Burnham. *(Stewart P. Evans)*

but decided not to stay because it lacked a bathroom. They eventually settled on an establishment run by Mrs Crossley at 16 Regent Road, which did have a bathroom. The rent was 10s a week.

Smith expressed concern for his wife's health to Mrs Crossley and Dr Billing was consulted. The long journey from the south coast to Blackpool had been an arduous and tiring experience for his wife: she had a headache. Dr Billing could find no cause except mild constipation. Smith persuaded Alice to write to her parents: 'My husband does all he can for me, in fact I have the best husband in the world.'

In the early evening, two days after their arrival in Blackpool, Mr and Mrs Smith went out for a walk. It was Friday 12 December 1913, the last night of Alice Burnham's life. The daughter of the landlady had agreed to prepare a bath for Mrs Smith, and the couple returned to their lodgings a little after 8 p.m. At 8.15 the Crossleys were sitting in their kitchen, which was under the bathroom, when they noticed water stains appearing on the ceiling and down one of the walls. They assumed the bath had run over. At that moment Smith appeared at the kitchen door in a breathless state. He had two eggs in his hands. He told Mrs Crossley, 'I've brought these for our breakfast.' Having been told about the water, Smith went upstairs and a few moments later was heard to call out, 'Fetch the doctor! My wife cannot speak to me!'

Dr Billing was sent for and after he had made his examination, he returned downstairs to where Joseph Crossley and his wife were anxiously waiting and told them, 'Oh, she is drowned – she is dead.' Mrs Crossley found the tragedy, and Mr Smith's apparent indifference to it, too much to cope with. She arranged for him to stay next door that night. The next day he returned to make the necessary arrangements. In the afternoon Smith played Mrs Crossley's piano and drank a bottle of whisky.

The inquest was held at 6.30 p.m. that evening and Smith wept throughout. The coroner's jury returned a verdict of accidental death. Much to Mrs Crossley's surprise and disgust, Smith arranged for as cheap a funeral as possible. Alice's body was placed in a plain deal coffin and given a pauper's funeral, which took place at noon on Monday 15 December. Mrs Crossley was outraged when Smith callously remarked, 'When they are dead, they are done with.' Smith left for Southsea shortly after the funeral. As he departed Mrs Crossley, who thought he was 'a very hard hearted man . . . I did not like his manner', shouted after him, 'Crippen!'

Smith sold all of Alice's belongings that had been left in their lodgings in Southsea and returned to Edith in Bristol. He also pocketed the £500 paid out on the life insurance policy he had taken out on Alice. Among other benefits, the proceeds he received as a result of his involvement with Alice Burnham enabled him to increase his annuity by £30 a year. Having settled matters concerning the affairs of yet another 'bride', Smith returned to Bristol where he spent Christmas with Edith and her family. He told Edith he had just returned from a profitable visit to Spain. Early in 1914 Smith and Edith visited London, Cheltenham and Torquay. Smith also paid a visit to Bath in June, where he adopted the pseudonym John Lloyd and first encountered the lady who was the most high-born and last of his 'brides'.

At the outbreak of the First World War on 4 August, Smith was staying with Edith in Ashley Road, Bournemouth. It was during this time that he, while dressed in white flannels, white boots and a boater, and listening to a band in the sea-front gardens, encountered a maidservant by the name of Alice Reavil. This time he called himself Charles Oliver James. She fell for his charms and they were married in Woolwich by special licence on 17 September. They went to London and took lodgings at 8 Hafer Road, Battersea Rise. He soon persuaded Alice to part with her £76 savings, which she withdrew from the Post Office. He then took her out, left her in some public gardens on the pretext of going to the lavatory, promptly went to their lodgings and took everything except the clothes she was wearing. He immediately went back to Edith in Bournemouth. He gave some of Alice's clothes to Edith, telling her that he had bought them at a sale in London. Smith and Edith then travelled to Bristol before he returned to what is believed to have been his final victim, the lady whom he had met in Bath in June that year.

Margaret (Peggy) Lofty was the 38-year-old spinster daughter of a long-deceased clergyman. He introduced himself to her as John Lloyd, estate agent. She was at that time a lady's companion, a position she undertook from time to time, working for various respectable elderly women in the Bristol area. Her employment in that capacity ended in July. Peggy lived in Bath with her sister and elderly mother. She had experienced a deep disappointment earlier that year when she discovered that her fiancé was already married. When Smith, in the guise of John Lloyd, appeared on the scene, she must have felt greatly relieved – perhaps she was not going to be 'left on the shelf' after all. He charmed her and told her he would return, and he was as good as his word.

On 15 December she left her home to go out for tea, but she never returned. She told none of her family about her intentions to marry Mr Lloyd. Perhaps her previous experience made her reluctant to do so, until the knot had actually been tied. Smith married Miss Lofty at Bath Register Office on 17 December, having visited London a few days previously to arrange accommodation. They left Bath immediately after the wedding ceremony and took the train for London.

On their arrival in London the Lloyds went straight to 16 Orchard Road, Highgate, where they intended to lodge. Smith had visited Mrs Heiss, the landlady, a few days previously. However, having had time for reflection following his visit, Mrs Heiss had had second thoughts about taking the

Margaret (Peggy) Lofty. *(Stewart P. Evans)*

Lloyds in. He had inspected the rooms and the bath. Mrs Heiss, a German lady, later commented, 'I did not like the way he asked about the bath. . . . He measured it with his eyes.' She remembered that he remarked that it was a bit small, then said, 'I daresay it is large enough for someone to lie in.' She did not like his manner and thought he might be a difficult man to deal with, and this was not a time to have added difficulties if they were avoidable – after all, being German in London in 1914 was not easy. So when the Lloyds called on 17 December, she told them that the rooms were not ready and turned them away, despite Smith's protests.

However, he was familiar with that area of London and found lodgings in which he and his new wife could spend their wedding night. They moved into two furnished rooms at 14 Bismarck Road. The road was – and still is, albeit with a different name – situated opposite the Whittington Hospital and traverses the hillside between Highgate Hill and Archway Road. Bismarck, like many German names, was deemed unpopular both during and in the aftermath of the First World War, and the title was altered to Waterlow Road. The house had a bath. Miss Louisa Blatch was the landlady. That evening Mr Lloyd took his wife to see Dr Bates at 30 Archway Road. Characteristically for Smith, the dutiful husband expressed his concern to the doctor about his dear wife's poor state of health. The following morning, Friday 18 December, the last day of Peggy Lofty's life, Smith took his new bride to a solicitor to make her will. Her life was already insured for £700. He also took her on a visit to the Post Office to withdraw her savings. She wrote to her mother informing her of her marriage. She described her husband as 'a thorough Christian man . . . I have every proof of his love for me. . . . He has been honourable and kept his word in everything. He is such a nice man.'

Shortly after 7.30 that evening Mrs Lloyd took a bath. Miss Blatch, who was ironing in the kitchen, heard splashing coming from the bathroom directly above. She also heard Mr Lloyd playing 'Nearer My God To Thee' on the harmonium in the Lloyds' sitting-room. Shortly after that the front door slammed. Miss Blatch said at the trial, 'I heard a sound from the bathroom. It was a sound of splashing. Then there was a noise as of someone putting wet hands or arms on the side of a bath, and then a sigh . . . a sort of sound like a child might make.'

About 10 minutes after Miss Blatch had heard the splashing the doorbell rang. When she answered it, Mr Lloyd was standing on the doorstep. He mentioned the key which she had given him, but which he had forgotten. He told her that he had been for some tomatoes for Mrs Lloyd's supper and asked if his wife was down from the bathroom yet. He called to her and when his wife didn't answer he went up the stairs. Then he called out to Mrs Blatch, 'My God! It's my wife! She doesn't answer! I do hope nothing has happened to her!' Naturally, when Mr Lloyd entered the bathroom he found that his wife was dead. He tried to resuscitate her but to no avail.

Mrs Lloyd, the former Miss Margaret Lofty, was buried on Monday 21 December and Smith was soon back in Bristol, where he spent Christmas with Edith. On 27 December 1914 an article appeared on page 11 of the popular Sunday newspaper the *News of the World*. It was headlined 'Found Dead in Bath, Bride's Tragic Fate on Day after Wedding'. Joseph Crossley, husband of the Smiths' landlady in Blackpool, and Charles Burnham from Buckinghamshire, Alice Burnham's father, read the account and thought it sounded suspiciously like the so-called accidental death of Mrs Alice Smith at 16 Regent Road, Blackpool, a little over two years previously on 13 December 1913. They reported the matter to both their local police and to Scotland Yard. Mrs Heiss of 16 Orchard Road, Highgate, the landlady who had turned the Lloyds away, also contacted the police. She remembered Smith's comments concerning the size of the bath when he had first inspected her premises.

The inquest was held on Saturday 1 January 1915. Once again the grieving husband displayed great emotion and he was, of course, exonerated of any blame. The verdict was accidental death. However, as a result of the information given to the police by Joseph Crossley, Charles Burnham and Mrs Heiss, Mr Lloyd was placed under close observation and the police travelled to various parts of the country making exhaustive enquiries during the four weeks that followed. The net was closing in on Smith. The police investigation revealed sufficient evidence to enable them eventually to amass an astonishing 264 exhibits to show to the jury at the trial, and no fewer than 112 witnesses were called.

On 4 January 1915 Smith, calling himself John Lloyd, called at 60 Uxbridge Road, Shepherd's Bush, to consult with his solicitor, Mr Davies. He instructed the lawyer to have his wife's will proved and to realise the proceeds of her life insurance policy. He was completely unaware of the enormous police investigation that was taking place. When Smith went to his solicitor's office in Shepherd's Bush on 1 February to prove the will, he was arrested outside the building by Chief Inspector Neil and two police sergeants. Having admitted that he was George Joseph Smith, who had married Alice Burnham, he was then charged with bigamy. That same day, Margaret Lofty's body was exhumed and examined by Dr Bernard Spilsbury who, following several high-profile cases, had become the Home Office's honorary pathologist. Dr Spilsbury later travelled to Blackpool and Herne Bay to examine the exhumed bodies of Alice Burnham and Bessie Mundy.

After Smith had been identified by Charles Burnham as the man who had married his daughter, he was remanded in custody. During several appearances at Bow Street Magistrates Court he shouted abuse at the witnesses and

lawyers. Following further police investigations Smith was charged on
23 March with the wilful murder of Bessie Mundy, Alice Burnham and
Margaret Lofty, although he was actually indicted only for the killing of
Bessie Mundy.

At the age of 43, George Joseph Smith stood in the dock at the Old Bailey
on Tuesday 22 June 1915. His trial lasted for nine days, concluding on 1 July.
He pleaded not guilty. During the case the sensational revelations reported by
the press acted as a diversion from the horrors that were occurring in the
trenches across the English Channel. The presiding judge was Mr Justice
Scrutton and the senior prosecuting counsel was Archibald Bodkin, who later
became Director of Public Prosecutions. Smith was defended by the
formidable Edward Marshall Hall KC. Smith satisfied the authorities that he
had no money and as a consequence Marshall Hall provided his services for
the maximum fee allowed by the Poor Prisoners' Defence Act, £3 5s 6d.
Archibald Bodkin, prosecuting, first addressed the jury: 'This case is of a very
grave character, and one to which you will give the most earnest attention in
the interests not only of the prisoner, but also of the public.' He then turned
his attention to the judge and told him he wished to discuss an important
point of law concerning the admissibility of certain evidence. Mr Justice
Scrutton directed the jury to retire while it was being argued.

This point in the case marked a landmark in English criminal law: a
precedent was set. Mr Marshall Hall knew from the documents in his brief
that Smith had married two other women who had both died in their baths,
having both previously made wills with Smith as sole beneficiary. To allow
this information to be admitted would give Smith virtually no chance of an
acquittal and Mr Bodkin wanted to present the evidence. Strong arguments
were proffered on both sides. Mr Bodkin maintained that the prosecution
was entitled to call evidence of any character tending to prove that this was a
case of killing by deliberate design and not by accident. He also suggested
that Smith had employed a 'system'. Mr Marshall Hall contended that the
evidence of a 'system' was admissible only where it was necessary for the
defence to set up a denial of intent. In this particular case, as the prosecution
had not put forward sufficient evidence to displace the primary presumption
of innocence in the prisoner, the inclusion of the evidence of the previous two
fatalities was not necessary. Having considered both arguments Mr Justice
Scrutton ruled that such evidence was admissible. He then recalled the jury
and informed them that they must not use this evidence to infer that the
prisoner was a man of bad character and infamous acts, but only to help
them to decide whether Miss Mundy's death was the result of an accident or
had been deliberately engineered by the accused. Mr Bodkin then outlined the
facts of the two additional fatalities for which he suggested that the prisoner
was responsible.

Edward Marshall Hall KC, MP, counsel for the defence. *(Author's collection)*

The evidence given by Dr Spilsbury made it even more difficult for Mr Marshall Hall to proffer his usually masterly defence. He stated that it would have been impossible for his client to have killed Bessie Mundy without leaving some evidence that suggested there had been a struggle or some marks of violence on her. He commented, 'If you tried to drown a kitten, it would scratch you, and do you think a woman would not scratch?'

In the witness box Dr Spilsbury said:

If a woman of the stature of Miss Mundy was in the bath in which she died, the first onset of an epileptic fit would stiffen and extend the body. In view of her height, 5 feet 7 inches, I do not think her head would be submerged during that stage of the fit. . . . After the seizure had passed the state of the body is that of relaxation. The body would probably be limp and unconscious. Bearing in mind the length of the body and the size of the bath, I do not think she would be likely to be immersed during the state of relaxation. . . . Dr French has described her legs straight out from the hips and the feet up against the end of the bath, out of the water. I cannot give any explanation of how a woman – assuming she had an epileptic seizure – could get into that position by herself.

Mr Marshall Hall had very little evidence at his disposal with which he could adequately defend Smith. He cross-examined Dr Spilsbury with regard to Miss Mundy clutching a bar of soap as she died, suggesting that this could indeed indicate that she had suffered an epileptic seizure. However, Dr Spilsbury was cautious in his reply: 'It's not impossible,' he agreed, before adding, 'but not very likely.' Dr Spilsbury's proven skills in forensic pathology, a relatively new form of criminal detection, seemed to allow little doubt in the minds of the jury, and his suggestion for the method of drowning Smith might have adopted added weight to the overwhelming amount of circumstantial evidence against him. Dr Spilsbury explained that the vagus nerve, which connects the brain to the heart, can be stimulated by a sudden rush of water into the nose and throat, sending a message to the heart to stop beating, and resulting in rapid unconsciousness and death. The position of the bodies in the baths in which they were found, and in particular that of Bessie Mundy, indicated to him exactly how Smith had brought about a quick death to his victims with little sign of struggle.

To prove Dr Spilsbury's theory Inspector Neil arranged for a demonstration in an ante-room at the Old Bailey. The inspector had a nurse, dressed in a bathing costume, sit in a bath of water, the bath being of a similar size and shape to those used by Smith. A police officer then demonstrated the technique suggested by Dr Spilsbury. He placed his right hand on the nurse's head and his left arm beneath both of her knees. The police officer then raised his left arm suddenly while at the same time used his right hand to press down on the head, pushing it beneath the water. As predicted, Dr Spilsbury's theory proved correct and a near-tragedy resulted. The nurse had to be revived using artificial respiration.

Mr Marshall Hall was up against mounting evidence, but he called on all the resources at his disposal. In particular he stressed the mutual affection between the prisoner and Edith Pegler, citing it as evidence of Smith's humanity. Of the 112 witnesses called at the trial, Edith was the only surviving 'bride' to give evidence. When she was on the stand Smith showed signs of distress. She told the court that the prisoner had on the whole been kind to her. She said that Smith had warned her of the danger women face when taking baths. She stated he had told her, 'I should advise you to be careful about these things, as it is known that women often lose their lives through weak hearts and fainting in the bath.'

In his summing up to the jury Mr Bodkin said:

In each case you get the simulated marriage. . . . In each case all the ready money the woman had is realised. . . . In each case the woman made a will in the prisoner's favour. . . . In each case the property could only be got at through the woman's death. . . . In each case there were enquiries about the bathroom. . . . In each case the prisoner is the first to discover the death. . . . In each case the prisoner is the person in immediate association with each woman before her death. . . . In each case the bathroom doors are either unfastenable or unfastened. . . . In each case there is the immediate disappearance of the prisoner.

Circumstantial evidence, perhaps, but convincing nevertheless.

Mr Justice Scrutton's summing up lasted almost an entire day and during it Smith interrupted several times, at one point shouting, 'You'll have me hung the way you are going on! – Sentence me and have done with it! . . . It is a disgrace to a Christian country! I am not a murderer – though I may be a bit peculiar.' The judge also made reference to contemporary events. He said,

Since last August all over Europe . . . thousands of lives of combatants, sometimes of non-combatants, have been taken daily, with no warning, and in many cases with no justification. . . . And yet, while this wholesale destruction of human life is going on, for some days all the apparatus of justice in England has been considering whether the prosecution are right in saying that one man should die.

The jury retired at 2.52 p.m. on 1 July and took just 22 minutes to find George Joseph Smith guilty. Before he passed sentence of death by hanging, Mr Justice Scrutton remarked,

Judges sometimes use this occasion to warn the public against the repetition of such crimes – they sometimes use such occasions to exhort the prisoner to repentance. I propose to take neither of these courses. I do not believe there is another man in England who needs to be warned against the commission of such a crime, and I think that exhortation to repentance would be wasted on you.

Pale-faced and sweating profusely, Smith gripped the dock tightly as the death sentence was passed on him. He then leaned over the dock and said to Edward Marshall Hall, 'I thank you Mr Marshall Hall, for everything you have done. I have great confidence in you. I shall bear up.' After sentence had been passed on Smith, Edith Pegler burst into tears as she left the Old Bailey.

An appeal was lodged, but dismissed. Smith was then removed to Maidstone Prison from Pentonville, where he had been incarcerated since his committal. It was there on a sunny morning, at 8 o'clock on Friday 13 August 1915, that he was taken across the prison yard to the execution shed and hanged by John Ellis. He was in a state of collapse on the scaffold and maintained that he was innocent of murder to the end. After the execution the body of George Joseph Smith was formally identified by Inspector Neil. It was then buried in a pit of quicklime within the confines of Maidstone Prison.

8

The Tragic Story of Ruth Ellis
and the
Killing of David Blakely

Hampstead, 1955

Very few criminal cases have attracted as much public attention and provoked such conflicting opinions as that of Ruth Ellis, the last woman in Britain to be hanged. Some less generous-spirited commentators have said that had this 'ice-cool' murderess not been a young woman with undoubted physical attractions, then the case would not have warranted so much media attention, nor indeed prompted the degree of public indignation following her conviction for murder and subsequent execution.

That she killed David Blakely was never in doubt and when the jury reached their verdict, Mr Justice Havers passed the only sentence available to him. She died at the end of a hangman's rope in the execution shed at Holloway Prison on 13 July 1955. Sadly, no posthumous reprieve, pardon or lessening of the severity of her crime could ever alter that fact, but campaigners have worked tirelessly for almost half a century to see her crime reduced to manslaughter. The most recent call to overturn her murder conviction, considered by appeal court judges Lord Justice Kay, Mr Justice Silber and Mr Justice Leveson in September 2003, was not successful. Lord Justice Kay delivered the judgement on 8 December 2003, dismissing the appeal as 'without merit'.

A little after 9 p.m. on Easter Sunday, 10 April 1955, a bleached platinum blonde wearing a grey two-piece suit and green sweater was seen peering through the window of the saloon bar of the Magdala Tavern in South Hill Park, a short distance from Hampstead Heath railway station. A customer, Alan Thompson (who within just a few short minutes was to play a significant part in events), noticed her from where he was sitting in the saloon bar. Having looked through the window, the young woman retreated and waited in the doorway of a newsagent's shop next door. Ruth Ellis had made her way to South Hill Park earlier that evening from her home at 44 Egerton Gardens, Kensington. As she waited she put on her black-rimmed spectacles.

Inside the Magdala Tavern were 25-year-old racing driver David Blakely and his friend, 30-year-old Mayfair car salesman (Bertram) Clive Gunnell. Blakely cashed a cheque for £5 with the landlord, Mr Colson. The two men stayed in the bar for about 10 or 15 minutes, according to Gunnell. They had a couple of drinks and Blakely purchased three flagons of beer before they left the pub to go back to the party they had left in nearby Tanza Road.

As they left the Magdala Tavern, Blakely carrying one flagon of beer, Gunnell carrying two, Blakely went to open the driver's door of his Vanguard, which was parked immediately outside the doorway, facing downhill with the driver's door nearest the kerb. As Blakely stood by the car, feeling for his keys in his pocket, two men standing nearby noticed a young blonde woman as she stepped out from the doorway of Hanshaw's newsagent. She called out, 'David'. Blakely did not answer, neither did he acknowledge that she was even there, but carried on searching his pockets for his keys while still cradling the beer he had bought just a few moments before.

As the woman drew up close to Blakely she swiftly put her hand into her handbag and drew out a .38 Smith & Wesson revolver. She did not utter another word but raised the gun and pointed it directly at Blakely. He turned and ran towards the front of the Vanguard to seek cover, but as he did so Ellis fired two shots into his back in quick succession. Blakely slumped into the side of the car, smearing it with blood, and reached out to his friend, who was standing rigid with astonishment, and called out, 'Clive!' Ellis pursued the stumbling Blakely round his car as he was attempting to make his escape. As she followed him she called out, 'Get out of the way, Clive.' She then fired another shot and as the bullet entered his body, Blakely contorted in agony and fell face down, with his head at the point where the Magdala Tavern met Hanshaw's, his left cheek on the ground. Ellis walked up to the now-motionless body and pumped more shots into it. She emptied the revolver, until all six rounds had been fired and the empty gun clicked as she continued to pull the trigger.

At least four of the six bullets tore through Blakely's body, causing considerable damage to his vital organs as well as massive shock and haemorrhaging. As Ruth fired the last bullet it missed Blakely, hit the pavement, ricocheted and struck the hand of a passer-by, 53-year-old Mrs Gladys Kensington Yule, who was walking to the Magdala Tavern with her husband. The bullet passed through her left hand at the base of the thumb before fragmenting and hitting the tiled wall of the pub. Witnesses said Ellis did not appear to notice Mrs Yule's cry of pain. The motionless body of David Blakely lay on the pavement surrounded by a mixture of blood, frothing beer and broken glass. Ellis, still holding the gun, said quite calmly to Clive Gunnell, who was holding his dying friend, 'Now go and call the police, Clive.' She stood trembling, with her back against the pub wall.

Inside the Magdala Tavern was the person who had seen Ruth Ellis peering through the window just a short while before. He was an off-duty policeman, Police Constable 389 Alan Thompson, of L Division of the Metropolitan Police. He was having a quiet drink while he waited for his girlfriend to arrive when someone rushed into the bar shouting, 'A bloke's been shot outside.' PC Thompson went outside to investigate. Ruth Ellis was standing with her back to the pub wall clutching the revolver in her right hand and still pointing it towards David Blakely. PC Thompson calmly walked up to her, took the gun and put it in his pocket. As he did so, Ruth said to him, 'Will you call the police?' He replied, 'I am the police.' 'Will you please arrest me?' she said. Ruth then received the first of three cautions delivered to her that night.

Officers were quick to arrive from nearby Hampstead police station. An ambulance was sent and Blakely was accompanied by Gunnell to New End Hospital, where he was pronounced dead on arrival. Mrs Yule's husband could not wait for an ambulance but summoned a taxi, whose driver agreed to take them to the hospital only on condition that she hold her blood-dripping hand out of the cab window to avoid staining the interior of his vehicle.

Accompanied by several burly policemen, Ruth Ellis (who stood just 5ft 2in tall) was taken to Hampstead police station in nearby Rosslyn Hill. There she made a statement that was witnessed by three senior CID officers from S Division – Detective Superintendent Leonard Crawford, Detective Chief Inspector Leslie Davies and Detective Inspector Peter Gill. Ruth Ellis was charged with murder at 12.30 p.m. on Easter Monday, 11 April 1955. The following day she made a brief appearance at Hampstead magistrates' court before being removed to Holloway Prison, where she became Prisoner 9656.

Ruth was born on 9 October 1926 at 74 West Parade in the North Wales seaside resort of Rhyl. Her father, Arthur Hornby, was a musician who used the professional name Arthur Neilson, and the name Neilson appeared on Ruth's birth certificate. Ruth's mother Elisaberta, more commonly known as Bertha, was half French and half Belgian. Ruth was the third of six children and from an early age was near-sighted and needed spectacles, although as she became more conscious of her appearance and adopted sophisticated tastes she seldom wore them.

In 1939 Arthur Neilson found work at Reading in Berkshire. The family went with him. Ruth left school in 1941 and later that same year her father found work as a chauffeur in London. The job brought with it a two-bedroomed flat and Ruth went to live there with her father. She found herself work in a munitions factory and then at a food-processing company. It was

Ruth Ellis. *(Keystone/Getty Images)*

during this period that she began to bleach her dark brown hair with peroxide. She spent her leisure hours at dance halls, cinemas, cafés and drinking clubs, although she was still only 16 years old. She was determined to enjoy herself, and nurtured hopes of improving her prospects and lifestyle by mixing with a 'better class' of people.

In March 1942 Ruth was taken ill with rheumatic fever. After her discharge from hospital she took the medical advice she was offered that dancing would help strengthen her body and aid recovery. She found a job as a photographer's assistant at the Lyceum Ballroom in London's West End. It was there in late 1944, at the age of 17, that she met and fell in love with a French-Canadian soldier. After a brief affair she became pregnant. The soldier promised Ruth many things but like thousands of similar wartime romances, all came to nothing. She gave birth to an illegitimate son on 15 September 1945 in a private nursing home at Gilsland, deep in the Northumbrian countryside. She christened him Clare Andrea Neilson – Clare was his father's name – but the boy was usually called Andy. On her return to London, Ruth turned to her sister Muriel for support. It was Muriel who could be relied on most and it was she who acted as surrogate mother to Andy in the years that followed.

In need of a job, Ruth got work as a model at a camera club. She soon found herself posing nude while the club's devotees snapped away. Occasionally, after work she would be invited out by members and taken to numerous drinking venues in the West End. It was in one such club that she met Maurice (usually known as Maury or sometimes Morrie) Conley, a wealthy businessman and nightclub owner.

Ruth met Conley at the Court Club, 54 Duke Street. He was impressed by her and decided that she had the right personality, charm and air of authority to operate as a good hostess. He offered her a job and Ruth joined six other hostesses. The pay was good; she also had a clothing allowance, free drinks and was able to mix with the 'better class' of people she yearned for. Ruth worked in various clubs owned by Conley over a nine-year period, but her advancement had its price and Ruth found herself obliged to offer various sexual favours. Early in 1950 she became pregnant by one of her regular customers. She had an abortion and returned to work almost immediately, but she began drinking heavily and in the summer of that year she met a man who was to become a major influence on her life. However, once again, he would turn out to be the wrong sort of man.

In June 1950 Ruth was working at the Court Club and a customer by the name of Ellis became very persistent in his attentions to her. He kept pestering her to spend the evening with him. Divorcee George Johnson Ellis was a dentist. He was musically talented and held a private pilot's licence, something of a rarity then. He was also a hopeless alcoholic. He was born on 2 October

1909 in Manchester and had two sons by his first wife Vera, but the marriage was not happy and his frequent bouts of heavy drinking led to mood swings. One day he returned home to Sanderstead to discover that his wife and children had left, taking with them the household furnishings. Afterwards he spent an ever-increasing amount of time in bars and clubs.

Ruth had heard about Ellis from the other hostesses who called him 'the mad dentist'. He was lavish with money and told outlandish stories about his exploits. Ruth had made other plans for the night and intended to go out partying. However, to get rid of Ellis she agreed to meet him later at another club owned by Conley, the Hollywood. She never turned up. The next day Ruth was mortified to discover that while Ellis was waiting for her outside the Hollywood, he had made approaches to a woman who, unbeknown to him, was with some East End gangsters from Bethnal Green. One of them attacked Ellis and slashed his face with a razor. When he appeared again at the Court Club, his face was stitched. Ruth felt sorry for him and agreed to go on a dinner date. She was chauffeur driven to Ellis's golf club at Purley Downs, and then wined and dined, before returning with Ellis to his house in Sanderstead, Surrey.

George was very generous where Ruth was concerned and showered her with gifts. He took her on a three-month holiday to Cornwall and on their return she moved into Sanderstead. By now he was hitting the bottle heavily and agreed to admit himself into Warlingham Park Hospital in Surrey, where he received treatment for alcoholism. Shortly after his release Ruth and George married at the register office in Tonbridge, Kent, on 8 November 1950. He found work at a dental practice at Southampton early in 1951 and they moved to Hampshire.

They often quarrelled. She left him several times but always returned, and the situation worsened – on more than one occasion the police had to be called. By May 1951 the dental practice had had enough of Ellis and he was asked to leave. He admitted himself to hospital once again for detoxification. Ruth visited him often, but she began to convince herself that he was having improper relations with the female staff and patients. During one visit she became so hysterical that she had to be physically restrained and sedated. The psychiatrist who was looking after her husband at that time, Dr T.P. Rees, prescribed drugs for her and she remained under his care until the day she killed David Blakely.

On 2 October 1951 Ruth gave birth to a 7lb girl at Dulwich Hospital. The baby was named Georgina. Ellis took a job as schools dental officer and moved to Warrington in Cheshire, but he filed a petition for divorce from Ruth on the grounds of cruelty. She now needed to find work urgently and turned to Maurice Conley, who was delighted to see her. He gave her a job at what had been the Court Club but was now Carroll's. The refurbished establishment now included a restaurant, cabaret and dancing and stayed open until 3.00 a.m. Conley arranged for Ruth to move into Flat 4 at Gilbert Court, Oxford Street, a block owned by his wife Hannah.

In December 1952 Ruth became ill, and during treatment it was found she had developed an ectopic pregnancy. After an operation she remained in hospital for two weeks, but by April 1953 she had returned to work. During the long, hot summer of 1953, not long before Ruth moved on from Carroll's, a new group of young people started using the club. They raced cars for a living and based themselves at the Steering Wheel Club, situated across the road from the Hyde Park Hotel, but they often came to Carroll's during the afternoon. One day in September Ruth had her first encounter there with David Blakely.

In October 1953 Conley offered Ruth the job of managing one of his clubs. Called the Little Club, it was situated at 27 Brompton Road, Knightsbridge. Unlike his larger establishments where there were many staff, the Little Club was more intimate. Ruth was to run the club with three staff and was given a two-bedroomed flat above it, £15 a week salary and £10 a week entertainment allowance. David Blakely was already a member there and he became one of Ruth's regular customers. The attraction that developed between them was to prove fatal for both parties.

Blakely was born in a Sheffield nursing home called Oakdale on 17 June 1929, the youngest of three sons and a daughter of Dr John and Mrs Anne Blakely. His parents divorced in 1940 and in 1941 his mother married again. Her new husband was a successful businessman, a millionaire and one of Britain's best-known racing drivers, Humphrey Wyndham Cook. David was sent to boarding school in Shrewsbury and then completed two years mandatory National Service in the army. His stepfather's influence then secured him work as a management trainee at the Hyde Park Hotel. Brown-eyed and with long, silky eyelashes, David Blakely stood 5ft 9in tall and weighed about 11 stone. In addition to his salary from the Hyde Park Hotel, he received money from his stepfather and an allowance from his mother, which enabled him to maintain a second-hand sports car. It was an HRG (named after the designer H.R. Godfrey), bought for him as a 21st birthday present by his stepfather. He entered it in various races and gained experience as a racing driver. Dr John Blakely, his father, died suddenly in February 1952 and David received £7,000 as his share of his father's estate.

He formed a relationship with a regular customer at the Hyde Park Hotel, Miss Linda Dawson, the daughter of a wealthy industrialist from Huddersfield, Yorkshire. He also had affairs with numerous other women, including an American model, a theatre usherette and Carole Findlater, the wife of his friend Anthony, whom he had first met in 1951 when Ant (the pet name by

David Blakely and his car. *(popperfoto.com)*

which Findlater was usually known) was trying to sell an Alfa Romeo sports car. David was sacked from his position at the hotel in October 1952 following an altercation with the banqueting manager, after which his mother took him away with her on a world cruise. On his return he joined a manufacturing company, Silicon Pistons of Penn in Buckinghamshire, conveniently near the new family home. Although he had use of a flat attached to this house, David preferred to spend his time at his stepfather's London home at 28 Culcross Street, Mayfair.

A little over a month after David first met Ruth Ellis, he became engaged to Linda Dawson, and an announcement to that effect appeared in *The Times* on 11 November 1953. This event did not prevent his sleeping with Ruth at her flat above the Little Club.

The affair between Ruth and David continued and at her trial Ruth stated,

In December 1953 I had an abortion by him and he was very concerned about my welfare. Although he was engaged to another girl, he offered to marry me and he said it seemed unnecessary for me to get rid of the child, but I did not want to take advantage of him. I was not really in love with him at the time and it was quite unnecessary to marry me. I thought I could get out of the mess quite easily. In fact, I did so with the abortion.

At the beginning of 1954 George Ellis reappeared on the scene. He visited Ruth at the Little Club and was pressing for their divorce to become final, but she stalled for time in order to keep the maintenance money he was paying. One problem was what should be done with their 3-year-old daughter Georgina. Ruth's living conditions and lifestyle were not conducive to bringing up a little girl, and after considerable deliberation it was decided that George should take the child back to Warrington to arrange adoption. This finally took place in May 1954.

In June 1954 David went to Le Mans to drive in the 24-hour race and returned in the middle of July; during the trip he sent Ruth two postcards. She, angry that her lover was away so long, had an affair with 32-year-old Desmond Cussen. Born in Surrey, Cussen had been an RAF pilot during the Second World War, flying Lancaster bombers. After demobilisation in 1946 he became an accountant and was later appointed a director in his family's business Cussens & Co., a wholesale and retail chain of tobacconists with branches in London and Wales. He was a car enthusiast and although he never raced professionally himself, he found companionship at the Steering Wheel Club. Cussens had met Ruth at Carroll's club, long before David Blakely came on the scene, and he and Blakely had no liking for each other.

When Blakely returned from France Ruth forgave him for being away so long. She arranged a 25th birthday party for him on 17 June 1954, but he arrived late. After explaining that he had been to the Hyde Park Hotel and that his engagement with Linda Dawson was over, he asked Ruth to marry him. Clearly Ruth was delighted and reassured at this offer, but it seems nothing ever came of the proposal, except that she decided to stop fighting the divorce proceedings brought by George Ellis.

Blakely raced at Zandvoort in Holland in August 1954 in an MG owned by a friend, and this time he invited Ruth to join him. She was pleased at the offer but decided not to go. For many months David had been occupying his spare time building a racing car he called 'The Emperor'. He paid Ant Findlater £10 a week to work on it, but building the car was a costly exercise; the money he made at the piston factory and the allowance his mother gave him hardly covered his expenses. He asked Ruth if he could move in with her. She agreed and also allowed him a slate at the club.

Both of them now began to drink heavily. In October Ruth hosted her 28th birthday part at the Little Club. Blakely sent her a telegram from Penn. Both parties had now become jealous of the other. Ruth had found out about

Blakely's affair with Carole Findlater and he was frequently violent towards her, often after he became jealous over incidents that occurred in the club bar – incidents he referred to as 'tarting around'. Ruth mentioned this at her trial.

Towards the end of the year takings at the Little Club had fallen from over £200 a week to less than £80. Ruth had let David run up a bar bill that he could never repay. Whether of her own volition or on Conley's request, Ruth left the Little Club during December 1954. Homeless and needing a place for herself and Andy to stay when he returned from boarding school for the Christmas break, she turned once again to Desmond Cussen, who allowed her to move in with him at his spacious flat at 20 Goodwood Court, Devonshire Street, Marylebone. She assured Blakely that she would not sleep with Cussen, and between 17 December 1954 and 5 February 1955 Ruth and David spent several nights at the Rodney Hotel, Kensington. She told Cussen that she was staying the night with girlfriends or visiting her daughter Georgina in Warrington. On Christmas Day 1954, Ruth hosted a party at Cussen's flat.

The following day David raced The Emperor for the first time at Brands Hatch in the Kent Cup, in which he came second. By early in the New Year Ruth had convinced herself that David was having another affair. She got Cussens to drive her to Penn. A little detective work ensued and Ruth saw David leaving the home of a good-looking married woman, older than himself, whose husband was away on business. She had a blazing row with him about the affair during a stay at the Rodney Hotel on 8 January and he subsequently left for Penn. Having heard nothing from him, Ruth sent a telegram on the 10th; it read: 'Haven't you got the guts to say goodbye to my face – Ruth.'

However, by 14 January David and Ruth were back together again in the Rodney Hotel and on that same day Ruth received her decree nisi – her divorce from George Ellis would be absolute in six weeks. The final obstacle would be removed and there was nothing to stop them marrying, but in the days that followed Ruth continued to suspect that Blakely was having an affair. On 6 February a major row took place in Cussen's flat while he was away. David called his friends Ant Findlater and Clive Gunnell, claiming that Ruth had tried to stab him. When they arrived they found a drunken Ruth with a black eye, limping and covered in bruises. David was also drunk, had a black eye and was limping. Ruth had David's car keys and she would not give them to him. She did not want him to leave and at one point she lay down in front of Gunnell's car. Eventually, after Ruth had sobered up, the three men left in Gunnell's car and Ruth went back to Goodwood Court.

When Desmond Cussen returned, she had him drive her around to look for David. They went to the Findlater's flat and then to the Magdala Tavern, a favourite drinking place for Blakely and his friends. Another journey took them to Euston, where Ruth tried to trace a woman Blakely had mentioned during one of their increasingly drunken brawls, and on to Penn and Gerrard's Cross, where David's car was seen outside a pub. An altercation took place and Blakely was in danger of being beaten by Cussen, but he took off for London before any damage was done. That afternoon Ruth received a bunch of red carnations. The accompanying card read: 'Sorry darling, I love you, David.'

When they met later that night Blakely explained his behaviour by saying that he was jealous because she was staying in Cussen's flat. They agreed to look for somewhere of their own, providing they could borrow some money. Cussen loaned them the cash, but Ruth kept him sweet by promising to visit from time to time and she kept a spare set of keys to his flat. On 8 February 1955 Ruth took out a lease on a flat at 44 Egerton Gardens, Kensington, a tall, red-brick building consisting of furnished and serviced rooms, managed by housekeeper Mrs Winstanley and situated near the Brompton Oratory. Ruth and Blakely moved in as Mr and Mrs Ellis.

On 22 February there was another row about the woman in Penn and Ruth sustained a black eye and severe bruising. In early March Ellis, Blakely and Cussens attended the British Racing Drivers' Club dinner and dance at the Hyde Park Hotel. She danced alternately with both of them. She retired that night to Egerton Gardens and David joined her, but the following morning she asked him to leave and for the next week she spent her time with Cussens. Ruth had decided on a change of career and Cussens, as well as buying her a new set of clothes, was financing her in a modelling course. He drove her there each morning and picked her up after her lessons were over.

In March 1955 Ruth was once again pregnant. She miscarried during the last week of that month after Blakely had been violent towards her and had punched her in the stomach. At her trial Ruth said, 'He only used to hit me with his fists and hands but I bruise easily. I was full of bruises on many occasions.' Exactly who the father of the child might have been is hard to determine.

Blakely entered The Emperor at a race meeting at Oulton Park, near Chester, which was due to take place on Saturday 2 April, and on 31 March he, Ruth and Ant Findlater drove to Cheshire where Blakely and Ellis booked into a hotel as Mr and Mrs Blakely. Unfortunately Blakely never got to drive The Emperor at the main meeting because the car broke down during one of the practice laps, but on the Saturday night David and Ruth held a party at their hotel. Carole Findlater had joined her husband the previous night and at the trial she recalled that David and Ruth argued constantly, he blaming her for jinxing his car and she telling him, 'I'll stand so much from you, David. You cannot go on walking over me forever.' To which Blakely replied, 'You'll stand it because you love me.'

On her return to London on Sunday night Ruth felt ill. She was feverish and had a temperature of 104 degrees. On Monday Cussens called to see her at Egerton Gardens and insisted she stay in bed while he went to pick Andy up from his boarding school for the Easter holidays. Andy came back to Egerton Gardens and slept on a camp bed in his mother's bedroom. Blakely visited her late in the evening on both Monday and Tuesday, telling Ruth he had been attending to matters concerning The Emperor. On the Wednesday he brought her a photograph of himself. It was a promotional picture produced for the Bristol Motor Company's works team – he had been selected to race in the Le Mans 24-hour race on 9 June. On it he had written, 'To Ruth with all my love, David.' In January Ruth had started taking French lessons, paid for by Desmond Cussen, because she wanted to surprise David with her linguistic skills when they went to the race. On the Thursday they had arranged to go to the theatre, but Blakely was late arriving at Egerton Gardens and instead they went to the cinema, where he kissed and caressed her and told her how much he loved her.

On the morning of Good Friday, 8 April, Blakely left Egerton Gardens at about 10 a.m. He told Ruth he had a meeting with Ant Findlater to discuss matters concerning The Emperor, and he had promised Ruth that he would not visit him at his home in Tanza Road without telling her. (Ruth did not trust Ant and she trusted Carole Findlater even less.) Before he left, Blakely and Ruth made plans to take Andy out the following day.

When Blakely had not returned to Egerton Gardens by 9.30 p.m., Ruth telephoned the Findlaters. Her call was answered by their 19-year-old nanny, who said there was no one at home. Ruth rang again later and spoke to Ant, who told her that David was not there, but she suspected from his voice that this was not the case. She called Cussens, who agreed to drive her to Tanza Road in his black Zodiac saloon. On her arrival at No. 29, Ruth rang the doorbell of the Findlater's flat repeatedly and banged on the door; nobody answered. Blakely's dark green Vauxhall Vanguard, registration OPH 615, was parked outside. It had originally been a van but David had partially converted it to a saloon by removing the metal side panels and replacing them with windows held in place by rubber strips. Someone in the house called the police, after Ruth, screaming and shouting abuse, set about the car and pushed in several windows. Ant Findlater appeared on the doorstep in pyjamas and dressing gown and Ruth demanded to see David. At that point a police inspector arrived on the scene. He tried to persuade Ruth to go home but she told him, 'I shall stay here all night until he has the guts to show his face!' After making another attempt to persuade her to leave, and unwilling to interfere in a domestic situation, the inspector left the scene.

Ruth spent some time walking around the Vanguard and watching the Findlaters' flat from various points. She had convinced herself that the

South Hill Park, Hampstead, a present-day view of the Magdala Tavern, externally unaltered since Ruth Ellis shot David Blakely there in 1955. The shop to the right was once Hanshaw's newsagent. Ellis waited in the doorway of Hanshaw's for Blakely to emerge from the Magdala. *(Paul T. Langley Welch)*

Findlaters were deliberately coming between her and Blakely, and that he must be having an affair with the Findlaters' nanny. Desmond Cussens finally drove her back to Egerton Gardens at about 2.30 a.m. Early next morning she was back in Tanza Road. As Ant Findlater and Blakely cautiously emerged from the flat at about 10.30 a.m. and drove off in the Vanguard, they did not notice Ruth watching them from a nearby doorway. She then returned home to Egerton Gardens and gave her son some money before sending him off alone to spend the day at the zoo. Next Ruth persuaded Cussens to drive her to Hampstead. She went to the Magdala Tavern but Blakely was not there. Later that evening she was back outside the Findlaters' flat and she could hear what sounded like a party going on inside. She convinced herself Blakely was there and that the Findlaters' nanny was the subject of his amorous attentions.

The next day, Easter Sunday, Blakely's friend Clive Gunnell brought his record player to the Findlaters' flat and the assembled company prepared themselves for yet another session of partying over the holiday weekend. At about 9.00 p.m. Desmond and Gunnell decided to go to the Magdala Tavern for a drink and to get some beer and cigarettes. They drove to the pub in

Blakely's Vanguard and as they pulled away from outside 29 Tanza Road, Ruth was just arriving. She watched the car disappear and then turned up outside the Magdala Tavern. Less than fifteen minutes later Blakely was lying dead, and shortly after that Ruth Ellis was taken into custody and charged with his murder. David Blakely's body was removed from Hampstead's New End Hospital and taken to Hampstead mortuary, where a post-mortem examination was conducted by pathologist Dr Albert Charles Hunt. The cause of death was recorded as shock and haemorrhaging as a result of gunshot wounds.

The trial of Ruth Ellis lasted a day and a half and began in the No. 1 Court at the Old Bailey on Monday 20 June 1955 before Mr Justice Havers. The prosecution was led by Christmas Humphreys, Mr Griffith-Jones and Miss Southworth; and the defence was conducted by Melford Stevenson QC, with Sebag Shaw and Peter Rawlinson. Against the advice of her defence, who wanted to create an entirely different impression, Ruth appeared in court in a tailored black suit with astrakhan collar and cuffs over a white blouse. Her freshly bleached hair was neatly coiffured, after special permission had been given by the governor of Holloway Prison, Dr Charity Taylor, and her face was meticulously made up. Instead of giving the appearance of a vulnerable, confused woman, a victim of agonising circumstances, the impression she created was quite the opposite. On the advice of her defence, she pleaded not guilty to the indictment of murder, but the decisive question later asked by prosecuting counsel Christmas Humphreys sealed Ruth's fate. He asked her: 'Mrs Ellis, when you fired that revolver at close range into the body of David Blakely, what did you intend to do?' Ruth's reply was: 'It is obvious that when I shot him I intended to kill him.'

In his opening address Melford Stevenson told the jury that he was going to invite them to reduce the charge of killing from murder to manslaughter on the grounds of provocation. He also said:

> The fact stands out like a beacon that this young man became an absolute necessity to this young woman. However brutally he behaved, and however much he spent of her money on various entertainments of his own, and however much he consorted with other people, he ultimately came back to her, and always she forgave him. She found herself in something like an emotional prison guarded by this young man, from which there seemed to be no escape.

Mr Justice Havers could not allow a change to the crime for which Ruth was being tried and gave a lengthy explanation of his reasons; he warned the jury that in view of the evidence it was not possible to return a verdict of manslaughter. He said that there was 'not sufficient material, even on a view of the evidence most favourable to the accused, to support a verdict of manslaughter on the grounds of provocation'. Melford Stevenson then said that in view of the judge's ruling it would not be appropriate for him to say anything more to the jury. In his summing up Mr Justice Havers reminded the jury once again that it was not open to them to bring a verdict of manslaughter. His concluding remark seemed to seal Ruth Ellis's fate: 'I am bound to tell you that even if you accept the full evidence it does not seem to me that it establishes any sort of defence to the charge of murder.' The jury of ten men and two women retired at 11.52 a.m. and returned after 23 minutes at 12.15 p.m. They found Ruth Ellis guilty of wilful murder. As Mr Justice Havers donned the black cap, Ruth Ellis stood unmoving. After sentence had been pronounced she replied, 'Thank you.'

There was an enormous public outcry at the verdict. The death penalty abolitionists vehemently expressed their opposition to hanging Ruth Ellis. The anti-abolitionists also had their day, one in particular. It was unfortunate for Ruth that the innocent passer-by she had injured on the night she shot David Blakely, the bank official's wife Gladys Kensington Yule, was herself in a highly stressed state, and she and her husband were on their way to the Magdala for a restorative drink. Just two days before, on Good Friday, Mrs Yule's son from a previous marriage had committed suicide. At the trial Mrs Yule stated that as she and her husband had walked down South Hill Park from their home in Parliament Hill towards the Magdala, she saw a woman and two men in the vicinity of the tavern. She heard five shots, two before Blakely fell and two after he fell, and the last shot hit her. Mrs Yule was a staunch anti-abolitionist. On 11 July 1955 the *Evening Standard* printed a letter expressing her feelings on the subject of a reprieve for Ruth Ellis. It ended,

> If Ruth Ellis is reprieved, we may have other vindictive and jealous young women shooting their boy friends in public and probably innocent blood on their hands. *Crime passionel* indeed! What if other countries would let her off from her just punishment? When has Britain followed the lead of others? Let us remain a law-abiding country, where citizens can live and walk abroad in peace and safety.
> (Mrs) Gladys K. Yule, Parliament Hill, Hampstead

Ruth decided against an appeal. She felt there was no point: there were no legal grounds on which to base one. Despite considerable public and media pressure and a petition containing 50,000 signatures requesting clemency, the Home Secretary Major Gwilym Lloyd George could find no grounds for reprieve and on Monday 11 July Ruth received notice of this fact from the governor of Holloway. Thirty-five members of London County Council delivered their plea for clemency to the House of Commons on Tuesday 12 July, but to no avail. On the Tuesday evening, the eve of the hanging, a large crowd gathered outside the gates of the prison. Some broke through a police cordon and banged on the prison gates, shouting out for Ruth to pray with them.

Inside preparations were being made for the execution. Ruth had been weighed so that the correct length of drop could be calculated. This was not an exact science, but to an experienced executioner such as Albert Pierrepoint (who hanged over 400 men and women over a 25-year period) it provided sufficient information to ensure that death was swift. The gallows had been tested that afternoon using a sandbag weighing exactly the same as Ruth; it had been left overnight on the rope to remove any stretch. At about 7 a.m. Pierrepoint and his assistant Royston Ricard reset the trap and coiled the rope up above it to leave the leather-covered noose dangling at chest height.

The following column appeared in the *Daily Mirror* on the morning of Wednesday 13 July 1955.

THE WOMAN WHO HANGS THIS MORNING
By Cassandra
It's a fine day for hay-making. A fine day for fishing. A fine day for lolling in the sunshine. And if you feel that way – and I mourn to say that millions of you do – it's a fine day for a hanging. . . . If you read this at nine o'clock then – short of a miracle – you and I and every man and woman in the land with a head to think, and a heart to feel, will, in full responsibility, blot this woman out. . . . At mid-day the grave will have been dug while there are no prisoners around and the Chaplain will have read the burial service after he and all of us have come so freshly from disobeying the Sixth Commandment which says thou shalt not kill. . . .

When I write about capital punishment, as I have often done, I get some praise and usually more abuse. In this case I have been reviled as being 'a sucker for a pretty face'. Well, I am a sucker for a pretty face. And I am a sucker for all human faces because I hope I am a sucker for all humanity, good or bad. But I prefer the face not to be lolling because of a judicially broken neck. . . . Oscar Wilde, when he was in Reading Gaol, spoke of 'that little tent of blue which prisoners call the sky'. The tent of blue should be dark and sad at the thing we have done this day.

Cassandra was the pen-name of William Connor (knighted 1966).

On the morning of her execution Ruth rose at 6.30 a.m. In her cell was the photograph of Blakely's grave she had requested some weeks before. She wrote a letter to Blakely's mother and one to her solicitor. In preparation for her execution Ruth was given a large brandy by the prison doctor, and she knelt in prayer before a crucifix on the cell wall as she was served with communion by the prison chaplain.

At a little after one minute to nine Albert Pierrepoint entered the condemned cell. He pinioned Ruth's hands behind her back with his special calf-leather strap. He then led her the 15ft to the gallows and positioned her on the trap. While he drew a white-cotton hood over her head, his assistant pinioned her legs with a leather strap. Pierrepoint then placed the noose over her head and it secured the hood. He adjusted the rope's suspension point about 1in in front of her lower left jaw, then quickly removed the safety pin from the base of the lever, and immediately pushed the lever away from him to release the trap. The whole process from Ruth's leaving the condemned cell took no more than 10 or 12 seconds. The prison doctor examined the body in the gallows pit to confirm life was extinct before the execution chamber was locked for the customary one hour. At 9.18 a.m. the execution notice was posted on the prison gates, and shortly afterwards the crowd of about a thousand began to disperse.

Ruth Ellis was the last woman to be hanged in Great Britain; she was also the fifth woman to be hanged at Holloway Prison and the sixteenth woman to be hanged in the whole of Great Britain during the twentieth century. Albert Pierrepoint commented in his autobiography *Executioner Pierrepoint*:

> When I left Holloway after the execution of Ruth Ellis, the prison was almost besieged by a storming mob. I needed police protection to get me through. I knew that I would have walked out of Strangeways [where a 40-year-old woman had just been reprieved] a week earlier into an empty street. At Euston Station a crowd of newspapermen were awaiting me. I shielded my face from the cameras as I ran for my train. One young reporter jogged alongside me asking, 'How did it feel to hang a woman, Mr Pierrepoint?' I did not answer. But I could have asked: 'Why weren't you waiting to ask me that question last year, sonny? Wasn't Mrs Christofi a woman too?'*

At 10 a.m. Ruth's body was removed to the autopsy room adjacent to the gallows pit. There pathologist Dr Keith Simpson performed an autopsy on the body, and, as well as noting that the stomach contained 'Small food residue, and odour of brandy', he mentioned that the 'Deceased was a healthy subject at the time of death.' The cause of death was given as 'injuries to the central nervous system consequent upon judicial hanging'. Shortly afterwards, at about noon, the body of Ruth Ellis was buried within the precincts of Holloway Prison.

---

*Mrs Styllou Christofi was hanged at Holloway seven months before Ruth Ellis. Her conviction for the brutal murder of her daughter-in-law attracted no public outcry.

Crowds gathered outside Holloway Prison on 13 July 1955, the day Ruth Ellis was executed. *(Hulton Archive/Getty Images)*

In 1970 the rebuilding of Holloway required that the bodies of five executed women be moved. Along with those of the Islington baby-farmers, Amelia Sach and Annie Walters (see Chapter 2), Edith Thompson, who arranged for her lover to murder her husband Percy (executed 1923), Styllou Christofi, who murdered her daughter-in law Hella (executed 1954, see Chapter 10), Ruth Ellis was exhumed. The other women were reburied in unmarked graves at Brookwood Cemetery in Surrey. Ruth's son Andy, then aged 26, received permission to have his mother's body interred at St Mary's Parish Church, Amersham, Buckinghamshire. The headstone erected over her remains bore the name Ruth Hornby, but the choice of Ruth's maiden name did not secure her final resting place the degree of privacy her family desired, and the grave attracted many visitors. The headstone was eventually removed. David Blakely lies buried 4 miles to the south in a churchyard at Penn.

The story of Ruth Ellis and David Blakely has continued to arouse considerable public curiosity. There is so much that remains unexplained about this tragic case, a story of love, uncontrolled passion, violence, jealousy

The grave of David Moffatt Drummond Blakely
(1929–55) in the tranquil churchyard of the ancient
Holy Trinity Church, Penn, Buckinghamshire. *(Paul T.
Langley Welch)*

and hatred. Why was Dr T.P. Rees, the psychiatrist under whose care Ruth Ellis remained,
not called to give evidence by the defence at
Ruth's trial? If she were suffering from the
effects of legally prescribed sedatives, combined
with alcohol, at the time she fired the gun that
killed David Blakely, it might have rendered her
incapable of making a rational decision. This
point was never raised or discussed in court
during her trial. When she was examined by
psychiatrists before her trial they decided that
she was sane. The question remains, was she
sane at the time she shot David Blakely?

Did Ruth Ellis intend to kill herself with that
last bullet she fired into the pavement, which damaged the thumb of Gladys
Yule? Perhaps she did, but changed her mind at the last moment. It has been
suggested that she was suffering from post-miscarriage depression at the time
of the shooting, after losing her baby ten days earlier. It has also been
suggested that Ruth was mentally ill, suffering from battered-wife syndrome
and post-traumatic stress disorder, a condition that was not recognised until
the 1980s.

There was tragedy for some of those left behind too. George Ellis killed
himself in the summer of 1958. He had recently lost his job and went to
Jersey, where he booked into La Chalet Hotel at Corbiere. On Saturday
2 August he killed himself by looping a rope round the sides of his bed head
and then around his neck. He suffered death by strangulation. Over thirty
years later Andy, Ruth's son, also committed suicide at his flat in Euston by
taking a cocktail of alcohol and drugs. Desmond Cussen died in Perth,
Australia, on 8 May 1991 from complications that resulted from a fall on
24 April. He died of pneumonia and multiple organ failure following fracture-
dislocation of the neck. He was 68. In December 2001 Ruth's daughter
Georgina died of cancer at the age of 50.

Outside the Magdala Tavern, on the tiled walls beneath one of the saloon-
bar windows, the holes from the fragmented bullet that struck the thumb of
Gladys Yule can still be seen. Plaques have occasionally marked the spot
where the murder occurred but have soon disappeared, unscrewed from the
wall by souvenir hunters or outraged local residents.

9

Death of a Playwright

KENNETH HALLIWELL AND THE MURDER OF JOE ORTON

Islington, 1967

On Wednesday 9 August 1967 at about 11.40 a.m. a chauffeur-driven car arrived outside 25 Noel Road, Islington, to take 34-year-old playwright Joe Orton to Twickenham Studios, where he was to discuss his film script for *Up Against It*. The driver got out of the car, went through the front door of No. 25 and walked up the stairs to Flat 4 on the second floor. He knocked on the door. There was no reply. He went downstairs and checked with his office and was told to try again. After two or three more attempts at knocking on the door, he decided to look through the letterbox. Having done so, he noticed the light was on in the hall and in the room beyond he could just see the head of a bald man from the nose upwards. The man appeared to be lying motionless on the floor. The chauffeur knew the man was not Mr Orton as he had driven him twice before. He went downstairs again and the police were summoned.

When officers broke into the flat – a cramped affair, just a studio with kitchen and bathroom – they found the naked body of the flat's owner, 41-year-old Kenneth Halliwell. There were blood splashes on his chest, head and hands. Nearby on a divan bed was his flatmate and lover, Joe Orton, wearing only a pyjama jacket. Orton had severe head injuries inflicted by nine hammer blows to the skull. A blood-stained hammer was lying on his chest on the counterpane that covered his body. Brain matter had been spattered on both the wall and ceiling.

On the desk in the room in which they died, Halliwell had left a note placed on top of a red leather binder that held Orton's diary. It read:

If you read this diary all will be explained.
KH
PS. Especially the latter part

Kenneth Halliwell was brought up in a large semi-detached house in Bebington, Wirral. His father was a chartered accountant. In September 1937, the month Kenneth started at Wirral Grammar School, his mother suffered a horrific death after being stung in the mouth by a wasp. Kenneth had been close to his mother, who had pampered him, but his father virtually ignored him. Halliwell tried all sorts of ruses to get his father's attention, including running away from home, but his father remained indifferent. Halliwell excelled at school, where his teachers said that he would have no trouble getting into Oxford or Cambridge, but he wanted to be an actor.

One morning Kenneth came down to the kitchen and found his father's body. Charles Halliwell had gassed himself. Kenneth turned the gas oven off and after shaving and making himself a cup of tea, he went to report his father's suicide to the neighbours. The money his father left him gave Halliwell a degree of financial security that would eventually see him through the Royal

25 Noel Road, Islington. The plaque between the windows marks the second-floor studio flat where Joe Orton lived with Kenneth Halliwell from 1960 to 1967. (*Paul T. Langley Welch*)

Academy of Dramatic Art (RADA) and enable him to purchase his own home in London.

Joe Orton was brought up in Leicester in a working-class household. He first met Halliwell when they were both students at RADA in 1951. Halliwell was seven years older than Orton, and prematurely bald. Soon after they met Orton moved into Halliwell's flat. They lived together from that point until the day they died. After graduating from RADA Orton found work as an assistant stage manager, then occasional employment as a jobbing actor. Halliwell's acting career never really took off. Orton was heavily influenced by Halliwell's apparent sophistication and intellect, and Halliwell took the easily influenced Orton under his wing. By the late 1950s they had all but abandoned any thoughts of acting and had decided on a literary career.

In 1959 Halliwell purchased the studio flat at 25 Noel Road that from 1960 would serve as a base to enable them to write. Collectively their output was prolific, and Orton eventually developed a unique style far removed from the pretentious scribblings of Halliwell. Once this partnership had been established, the support that each gave the other was to reach fruition in Orton's success as a dramatist. This close relationship was cemented during the period when homosexuality was still a crime.

Often bored with their lack of success at getting their work published, and to anaesthetise themselves from the sometimes tedious jobs they were obliged to take, they made mischief to amuse themselves. In 1962 Orton and Halliwell were arraigned at Old Street magistrates' court for stealing seventy-two books from Islington and Hampstead libraries, and wilfully damaging a number of them. The allegations included the removal of 1,653 plates from art books (many of which adorned the walls of the flat, forming part of Halliwell's extensive collages) and adapting the designs of various book jackets (sometimes with hilarious results, although the magistrates did not see it that way). Orton also had a penchant for writing false (and often very crude) blurbs. Among his favourite targets were the Gollancz editions of Dorothy L. Sayers's Lord Peter Wimsey stories, which had blank yellow flaps.

The total value of the damage to the library books was estimated at £450. They were each given a prison sentence of six months. They were first taken to Wormwood Scrubs and then separated, serving their time in different open prisons, Orton in HM Prison Eastchurch and Halliwell HM Prison Ford Arundel. In his diary he wrote: 'I was locked in my cell for twenty-three hours a day. I used to have half an hour's exercise in the morning and half an hour in the afternoon. Now this didn't worry me so much, but it worried a lot of other people. I used to read a lot.'

On their release they resumed writing. Everything Joe Orton might have hoped for regarding the launch of his career as a successful playwright came about in 1963 when his work began to be taken seriously. Orton's originality as a dramatist was his uncanny ability to take taboo subjects and thoroughly offensive characters and make them palatable. Through humour he skilfully guided his audience around previously unthinkable territory. *Entertaining Mr Sloane* opened at the New Arts Theatre on 6 May 1964 and transferred to Wyndham's Theatre in the West End on 29 June, before moving on to the

18—N. London Press May 18, 1962

Ruined art books

A ROOM in Noel Road, N.1, shared by two men described as frustrated actors and authors, was said at Old Street on Tuesday to be covered from ceiling to floor with art plates "obviously taken from books from the public libraries." In one picture a monkey's head was pasted in the centre of a rose.

The men, Kenneth Leith Halliwell, aged 35, invoice clerk, and John Kingsley Orton, aged 29, lens cleaner, were told by the magistrate (Mr. Harold Sturge): "What I am anxious to see is that the decision of this court should make it abundantly clear to those who may be clever enough to write criticisms in other people's books—public library books—or to deface them or to ruin them in this way are made to understand very clearly that it is disastrous."

The magistrate added: "I am most concerned about the malice shown by you both in what you did—sheer malice towards fellow-users of this library who, until these books are replaced, will be denied what they might reasonably have expected to enjoy."

Both men pleaded guilty to seven joint charges—two of stealing library books, worth £48, 36 from the Essex Road branch and 36 from the Holloway Road branch—and five of damaging books to the extent of a total of £158. The last two of the seven charges referred to a total of 1,463 plates removed from library books.

Sentences of six months' imprisonment were passed on the first five charges, and fines of £2 or one month's imprisonment on the last two charges. All the sentences were concurrent.

Mr. William Hemming, counsel for the prosecution, said it was a most unusual and difficult case.

Counsel referred to a "quite lovely book." — Collins' "Guide to Roses." On the frontispiece a picture of a monkey's head had been pasted in the middle of a rose.

Referring to a book entitled "Discovery of Art," Mr. Hemming said: "On the front, where there should be pictures of eminent persons, there are the faces of cats, and a bird has been pasted where the face of an eminent person should be."

Det.-Sgt. Henry Hermitage said Halliwell had been employed as an actor. Orton, who asked that a further case of stealing six books from a Hampstead library should be taken into consideration, had attended R.A.D.A.

An article that appeared in the *North London Press* on 18 May 1952 concerning the library books defaced by Orton and Halliwell. (*North London Press*)

Queen's Theatre on 6 October; and *Loot* was produced soon afterwards. Orton's success attracted considerable media attention and started him on a meteoric rise that placed him at the forefront of the new-wave theatre world of the swinging sixties. He was much in demand at social gatherings. At first Halliwell basked in Orton's success and joined in with it, but gradually the pair grew apart and as Orton's escalating lack of dependency on his long-term lover became all too apparent, Halliwell's jealousy and paranoia began to surface.

It became increasingly, and all too painfully, clear to Halliwell that Orton's success was leaving his own pitiful efforts in the shade. It became evident that he would never be able to match the raw talent that Orton had honed to become one of the leading lights of the theatre world. In the homosexual scene in which Halliwell and Orton had circulated almost exclusively until recently, there had been no problem with Halliwell's place in Orton's life. But the more sober establishment found it difficult to accept Halliwell. He gave the impression of a man with more pretensions than talent. Too wooden as an actor and with his writing skills never quite reaching the mark, the only part of his life he seemed to have developed into anything approaching an

Orton goes over the script of the first production of *Entertaining Mr Sloane* with Dudley Sutton (Sloane) and Madge Ryan (Kath), 1964. *(Orton Estate)*

Orton, Kenneth Williams and Halliwell in Tangier, 1965. *(Orton Estate)*

acceptable art form was collage. The studio flat in which the couple lived was covered from floor to ceiling in Halliwell's collages. He attached great significance to his efforts in this field and once wrote to Peggy Ramsay, Orton's literary agent, to ask her opinion about them. John Lahr mentions this in his biography of Orton, *Prick Up Your Ears*. Halliwell wrote:

> I should like your opinion of my collage murals. Does my real talent if any lie in this direction, etc. . . . For instance the woman who came to interview J for the *Evening Standard* this afternoon spent her time admiring my murals and saying did they cost a terrific lot of money and how professional they were, etc. This has happened before with all sorts of people.

Halliwell lacked the self-assurance to try to promote himself and advance his efforts in this field, but Orton encouraged him and, in 1967, arranged an exhibition of fifteen pictures in Chelsea. A few were bought by Orton's business associates but the general public showed no interest whatsoever.

Unlike Orton, who enjoyed a highly varied sex life with a large number of partners, Halliwell was by comparison less promiscuous. Orton used to tease Halliwell about his lack of success in attracting both men and boys, and poked fun at his less than adventurous approach to all things sexual. Not only were Halliwell's meagre artistic efforts being overshadowed, which caused him no

Halliwell in 1967. Orton is sunbathing in the background. *(Orton Estate)*

small degree of anxiety, but he was also failing miserably in the most intimate part of his life. To add to the anxiety and self-doubt, Halliwell was very self-conscious about his baldness and kept his hat on everywhere he went, including the theatre. In an attempt to help him overcome this, Orton bought Halliwell a wig out of the money he made from *Entertaining Mr Sloane*.

Halliwell's bouts of depression grew deeper and more frequent. The diaries kept by Orton, which span the relatively short period from December 1966 to August 1967, chronicle not only his literary success, culminating in an *Evening Standard* Drama Award, but also give a candid account of his sex life both with Halliwell and numerous casual men, often describing exploits in the most unusual circumstances and unlikeliest of places. He also mentions Halliwell's black moods, which were becoming more frequent, his violent outbursts and his rapid decline into self-doubt. The entry for Monday 1 May 1967 reads:

> Kenneth H. had a long talk about our relationship. He threatens, or keeps saying, he will commit suicide. He says, 'You'll learn then, won't you?' And 'What will you be without me?' We talked and talked until I was exhausted. Going round in circles. Later I went out and bought some haddock for the dinner tonight.

In the entry for Friday 5 May Orton comments:

> When I got back home, Kenneth H. was in such a rage. He'd written in large letters on the wall, 'JOE ORTON IS A SPINELESS TWAT'. He sulked for a while and then came round. He'd been to the doctor's and got 400 valium tablets. Later we took two each and had an amazing sexual session.

On Monday 17 July:

> Kenneth v. irritating today. Weather hot again. Blue skies. Kenneth's
> nerves are on edge. Hay fever. He had a row this morning. Trembling
> with rage. About my nastiness when I said, 'Are you going to stand in
> front of the mirror all day?' He said, 'I've been washing your fucking
> underpants! That's why I've been at the sink!' He shouted it out loudly
> and I said, 'Please, don't let the whole neighbourhood know you're a
> queen.' 'You know I have hay fever and you deliberately get on my
> nerves,' he said. 'I'm going out today,' I said, 'I can't stand much more of
> it.' Go out then,' he said, 'I don't want you in here.' I went to Boots for
> the enlargements of the holiday snaps. They'd merely duplicated them,
> not enlarged them. So I had to take them back. Long face from Kenneth.
> 'I should've taken them myself,' he said, 'and why did you pay for them?'
> I took *What the Butler Saw* to Peggy. She looked at the title and said,
> 'Oh! It's just like the title of an old farce!'

The situation continued to deteriorate at home, but in his professional life
further success was on the horizon. The diary entry for Sunday 23 July reads:

> Yesterday morning Peggy rang me. Quite early. She'd read *What the
> Butler Saw* in a hotel room in York late on Thursday night. 'People
> must've thought I was mad,' she said. 'I simply had hysterics. It's the very
> best thing you've done so far.'

Orton made his last diary entry on Tuesday 1 August:

> Said goodbye to Kenneth this morning. He seemed odd. On the spur of
> the moment I asked if he wanted to come home to Leicester with me. He
> looked surprised and said, 'No.'

Throughout the pages of his journal Orton meticulously catalogued his day-
to-day existence in a frank and open manner. His sexual exploits and feelings
towards his friends, associates and acquaintances are all made clear. Orton's
obvious fondness for Halliwell is apparent, as is his deep concern for
Kenneth's mental health and their deteriorating relationship. Halliwell had
easy access to these diaries and as he read them it must have become apparent
to him that as his partner's rise continued, Orton was slipping away from him.
It seems Halliwell was not prepared to let that happen. To prevent Orton
leaving, Halliwell took a hammer and killed him as he rested on his bed. So
ended the life of one of the most gifted and finest post-war English
playwrights.

At the inquest evidence was given by Halliwell's doctor, Dr Douglas Ismay. The doctor said that Halliwell had made a previous suicide attempt seven years before, and had spoken to him about a holiday he had taken in Morocco with Orton earlier in 1967. Halliwell told Dr Ismay that while on holiday he had taken large quantities of hashish and had been eating it. Dr Ismay had arranged for Halliwell to see a psychiatrist.

Pathologist Professor Francis Camps, said, 'I doubt that he knew he was being hit. There is nothing to suggest any sort of defence.' Having inflicted horrific injuries on Orton, Halliwell took a massive overdose of barbiturates. He emptied the twenty-two capsules of Nembutal into a bucket and mixed it with a tin of grapefruit juice, which speeded the powerful drug into his system and caused death very quickly. Professor Camps said: 'From the fact that there was more of the drug in his liver blood than in his arms he died quite suddenly and did not simply become unconscious.' When the police broke into the flat Halliwell's body was cold but Orton's, although life was by then extinct, was still warm. Douglas Orton identified his brother and Orton's literary agent, Margaret (Peggy) Ramsay, identified Halliwell. Deputy Coroner for St Pancras, Dr John Burton, recorded the jury's verdict that Mr Orton, aged 34, was murdered by Mr Halliwell, aged 41, who then took his own life.

From 1967 the term 'Ortonesque' became part of the British vocabulary, a recognised description of 'macabre outrageousness'. Kenneth Halliwell's funeral took place at Enfield Crematorium on 17 August. It was attended by Peggy Ramsay and three of Halliwell's relations. Joe Orton's funeral took place at the West Chapel, Golders Green Crematorium, the following day. The funeral was arranged by Peggy Ramsay and Peter Willes of Rediffusion's Drama Department. It was a subdued gathering attended by Orton family members and the cast of *Loot*. As Orton's coffin, draped in a maroon pall and covered in red roses, was carried into the chapel, a tape recording of the Beatles' 'A Day In The Life' from their album *Sergeant Pepper's Lonely Hearts Club Band* was played; it was Orton's favourite song. Donald Pleasance read his own poem, 'Hilarium Memoriam J.O.'. Then Orton's friend Harold Pinter spoke a few lines and as the coffin slid away through the bronze doors, the chapel emptied to the sound of Debussy's 'Clair de Lune'. In the Arcade seventy wreaths had been laid out. A card on an iron stand bore the inscription 'Floral tributes for Mr Joe Orton'.

At Halliwell's funeral one of his relatives proposed that his ashes be mixed with Orton's. Peggy Ramsay suggested this to Joe's brother, Douglas. He agreed but added, 'As long as nobody hears about it in Leicester.' The ashes were mixed together and buried in the garden of remembrance at Golders Green Crematorium.

10

A Miscellany

MURDER IN MILLFIELD LANE, 1814

In 1814 Millfield Lane was a narrow thoroughfare, just as it still is today. It runs through Ken Wood and along part of the eastern edge of Hampstead Heath, adjacent to Highgate Ponds. There, on the floor of the kitchen in a cottage known as Millfield Farm Elizabeth Buchanan was found dead on 4 October. She was a washerwoman and was also known as Elizabeth Dobbins. Her 'husband' (they never actually married but had lived together as man and wife for many years) Mr Dobbins, who worked as a turncock for the Hampstead Water Company, was summoned by neighbours who suspected something was amiss when, looking through the kitchen window, they spotted blood on the floor. When he arrived, Dobbins discovered Elizabeth's body. She had been attacked and savagely beaten about the head with a poker, which had been left nearby covered with blood and bent with the force of the blows.

At about the same time a vagrant called Thomas Sharpe had been apprehended as he retreated furtively towards Highgate Hill carrying two bundles of washing stolen from the Dobbinses. He told a highly implausible story that he had bought the bundles from a gypsy. However, several witnesses testified that they had seen Sharpe in the vicinity of Millfield Farm. Sharpe already had a police record. At his trial Lord Ellenborough, having passed the death sentence, concluded with the words 'and may the Lord have mercy on your soul'. Sharpe replied 'May the curse of God attend you day and night, both in this world and the next.'

A SHOOTING IN HORNSEY WOOD, 1842

In May 1842 the population of North London was shocked when a police officer was murdered in the line of duty. At that time Hornsey Wood covered what is now the park itself in the part of the capital known as Finsbury Park. A hostelry known as the Hornsey Wood Tavern once stood close to the site of the present-day boating pond. Near this pub on 5 May 1842 Thomas Cooper, a 22-year-old bricklayer-turned-thief, was surprised by policeman Charles Moss while he was engaged in some felonious act. Without hesitation Cooper shot and wounded Moss. The noise of gunfire attracted the attention of

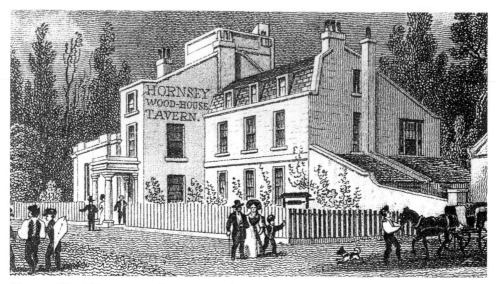

Hornsey Wood Tavern, seen here in an early nineteenth-century engraving. It was close to this spot that Thomas Cooper shot policeman Charles Moss on 5 May 1842. *(John D. Murray)*

another policeman called Mallet, and a baker called Mott who was walking in the woods nearby.

Mallet and Mott gave chase as Cooper headed off in the direction of Highbury. Meanwhile, another baker, named Howard, was driving his poste chaise down Hornsey Road. He saw Cooper being chased by Mallet and Mott and raced after him. Cooper headed for Highbury Barn. As another policeman, Timothy Daly, closed in on Cooper near Highbury Cottage, Cooper jumped over a hedge into a short cul-de-sac called Black Ditch. This area was bounded by a paling fence which hemmed Cooper in long enough for Daly and Howard to catch up. Cooper, who was carrying two large horse pistols, fired both of them. One hit its target and Daly died instantly, but Hudson was unscathed and with the help of two gardeners was able to overcome Cooper and hold him.

Cooper was tried, found guilty of murder and duly hanged.

THE SLAYING OF A RIVAL, PRIMROSE HILL, 1845

On 23 February 1845 a murder took place not far from the spot where Sir Edmund Berry Godfrey's body was discovered almost a hundred and sixty-seven years earlier (see Chapter 1). A policeman on patrol near the bridle path that ran through the fields between Primrose Hill and Belsize Park heard cries of 'murder'. When he arrived at the scene he found the bloody and battered body of a well-dressed man. The man appeared to have been robbed, because the only item found on his corpse was a letter written in blue ink and addressed to J. Cooper. The letter began 'Dear James' and in it the writer requested a meeting at their usual place; she also informed him that she was pregnant. It was signed Caroline.

About 20 minutes after the policeman arrived, a man called Thomas Hocker appeared at the scene of the crime and gave what assistance he could. After waiting until more help arrived, he left the scene. At no time did he indicate that he knew the victim, although it would become clear later that in fact he knew him very well.

Thomas Hocker, aged 22, and his close friend James De La Rue, aged 27, were a pair of amorous aspiring gentlemen, who had a penchant for collecting pornography in the form of prints which were readily available to those who knew where to acquire them. The pair of would-be Don Juans had developed acquaintances with numerous women, mostly servant girls and those who, although not exactly prostitutes, had loose morals: the type politely referred to as 'ladies of easy virtue'. Neither Hocker nor De La Rue could be described as either virtuous or honourable. Neither had any intention of cementing any of their relationships by marriage. Nor did they wish to become embroiled in paternity suits, and to that end they both used false names in their liaisons.

Of the two men, De La Rue was the most comfortably off. He earned his living as a piano teacher and was much in demand. He lived in well-appointed lodgings at 55 Whittlebury Street. The road no longer exists but in 1845 it led into Euston Square from Drummond Street, which straddles Hampstead Road. Hocker was not as well placed as his companion. Although he considered his musical talents to be worthy of more, he scraped a living by giving the occasional violin lesson. He lived at 11 Victoria Place, situated near the western edge of Regent's Park, and shared a room with his brother.

During the police investigation that followed, the deceased was identified as James De La Rue. Hocker's family were appalled at his apparent indifference to his best friend's death. Naturally they were questioned and as matters unfolded, Hocker's brother was able to give information about the 'Dear James' letter, which was written in one of Hocker's numerous false hands. The unusual blue ink was traced to Hocker's room, and this evidence, together with the discovery of De La Rue's watch and a pair of blood-soaked trousers, proved sufficient to convict him of De La Rue's murder. It transpired that the two men had quarrelled over a romantic attachment and Hocker, having made his plans and written the letter to lay a false trail, lured De La Rue to a remote spot, killed him and robbed him of his money and watch.

THE CASE OF MRS PEARCEY, KENTISH TOWN, 1890

The next North London murder to have an impact on the sensibilities of the late-Victorian public occurred in 1890. Mrs Pearcey, as this particular murderess preferred to be known, was in fact not married. Her real name was

Mary Eleanor Wheeler, but after she went to live with a man named Pearcey, she assumed his name and the title of his wife. Pearcey left her but she retained the surname until the day she died.

By the beginning of 1890 24-year-old Eleanor Pearcey was emotionally unstable, depressed and lonely. She had few relatives, just an elderly mother and an older sister, and often drowned her sorrows with strong drink. However, she was tolerably good looking and certainly attractive enough to inspire an admirer, Mr Chrichton of Gravesend in Kent, to pay for her three rooms in a house at 2 Priory Street (now Ivor Street), Kentish Town. He called on her once a week.

Another admirer was a furniture remover called Frank Hogg. She really loved this man and would place a light in her window to let him know when she was free. But Hogg used to see other women and one of his lady-friends fell pregnant; this woman, whose name was Phoebe, was known to Mrs Pearcey. He was pressured, if not forced, into marrying 31-year-old Phoebe by her family and in due course she was delivered of a baby girl, also called Phoebe. The marriage was not a happy one and Frank used to pour out his woes to Eleanor Pearcey, who became jealous of Phoebe Hogg and developed a deep hatred of her.

Frank and Phoebe Hogg lived in rooms at 141 Prince of Wales Road, Kentish Town. On Thursday 23 October 1890 Mrs Hogg received a note from Mrs Pearcey inviting her to tea. Mrs Hogg couldn't make it that day as she had prior commitments, but when another note arrived the following day, she went along to Priory Street, leaving home at about 3.30 p.m., and pushing little Phoebe in her bassinet. It seems that within minutes of her arrival Mrs Hogg was murdered by Mrs Pearcey. Neighbours later reported that they had heard 'banging and hammering' at about 4 p.m., and Phoebe Hogg had been killed with a poker and more than one knife. She had clearly put up a struggle as both her arms were bruised and, as was later discovered, so were Mrs Pearcey's. Mrs Hogg's throat had been so savagely cut that her neck had been all but severed.

That evening Mrs Pearcey put the body of Mrs Hogg into the bassinet on top of the baby. The baby had either already been suffocated or was suffocated by the weight of her mother's body. Mrs Pearcey then covered the top of the pram with an antimacassar and pushed her heavy load into Chalk Farm Road. She turned up Adelaide Road and into Eton Avenue, continuing her journey until she reached a partly built house in Crossfield Road, near Swiss Cottage. There she unloaded Mrs Hogg. Mrs Pearcey continued to push the bassinet along the Finchley Road where she disposed of little Phoebe on some waste ground. She then pushed the bassinet for another mile or so before abandoning it in Hamilton Terrace, an elegant street situated between St John's Wood and Maida Vale.

Mrs Hogg's body was soon discovered and the baby was found the following day. It was not long before the finger of suspicion was wagging at Mrs Pearcey. When the police went to her home they were astonished: she ascribed the bloodstains in the kitchen to killing mice and calmly sat at the piano humming a tune.

Eleanor Pearcey was tried at the Old Bailey on 1 December. The trial lasted for four days. Found guilty, she was hanged at 8 a.m. on Tuesday 23 December 1890 at Newgate by executioner James Berry. On Wednesday 24 December *The Times* reported:

> A drop of 6ft was allowed, and death was instantaneous. The convict said to Mr Duffield, the chaplain, as she was being led to execution, 'The sentence is just, but the evidence was false.' This was her only confession; to all others who saw her she repeatedly protested her innocence.

SHE KILLED HER SON, STOKE NEWINGTON, 1899

By 1899 the once isolated, elegant and picturesque village of Stoke Newington had become just another suburb surrounded by the urban sprawl of London. Louise (or Louisa) Josephine Masset, an attractive-looking woman, the daughter of a Frenchman and an English woman, was a resident there. She was 36 years old and earned her living either as a governess or as a piano teacher. She was unmarried and boarded at her sister's at 29 Bethune Road.

She had a 4-year-old son, Manfred Louis, whom she lodged separately with a foster mother in Clyde Road, Tottenham. The child was the result of an affair she had had in France, although his father's name was never divulged. In Stoke Newington Louise began having an affair with a neighbour, student Eudore Lucas who was also a Frenchman. As the affair grew stronger, Louise began to realise that Manfred was coming between her and her love life, and as a result Eudore's ardour was waning. If she was to retain his affection, Manfred could no longer be part of her life. She informed Manfred's foster mother that his father was going to take over the boy's upbringing in France and collected him on the morning of 27 October, along with a parcel containing his clothes. Louise Masset was last seen with her little boy at London Bridge station. Later that same day his battered and naked body was found wrapped in a black shawl in the ladies' lavatory on Platform No. 3 at Dalston Junction station. Nearby was a bloodstained stone that had been used to kill him.

After reading a report about the dead child in a newspaper, the foster mother came forward and identified him. Louise Masset was questioned by the police. She told them that she had handed her son over to two ladies at London Bridge who were opening a new orphanage in Chelsea. She had then caught a train to Brighton, where she had spent the weekend in the company of her lover. However, a paper parcel containing Manfred Masset's clothes was found in the waiting room at Brighton station, and the black shawl in which the boy's body had been found was identified as having been bought by Louise Masset at a shop in Stoke Newington. The stone used to kill the boy fitted a hole in the rockery in the garden at 29 Bethune Road.

The fact that this uncaring mother had killed her son and then immediately gone to Brighton to spend the night with her lover appalled and shocked the public, who could find no grain of sympathy for her. There was no outcry when Louise Masset was hanged at Newgate on 9 January 1900. She was the first person to be hanged in Britain in the twentieth century. The executioner was James Billington.

THE SMELL UNDER THE STAIRS, QUEENS PARK, 1904

In 1904 William Dell rented part of a house from George Crossman in Ladysmith Avenue (later renamed Wrentham Avenue), a short road running between Chamberlayne Road and Tiverton Road, Queens Park. He complained to Mr Crossman about an appalling smell that was coming from a cupboard under the stairs. Crossman told Mr Dell that it was a box of size (a gelatinous solution used, among other things, to prepare plastered walls for decoration) which had gone bad, and said he would arrange to have it removed.

Mr Dell was not convinced by Crossman's explanation and thought there was something sinister occurring, so he mentioned the matter to the police. Crossman arranged for men to carry the trunk away, and as they did so he puffed on a cigar, presumably in an attempt to cover up the disgusting smell. Just as the workmen were removing the trunk a policeman happened to call and expressed an interest in its contents. Crossman panicked and ran off, leaving behind a bemused policeman, Mr Dell and the men engaged to take the trunk away. They followed him, but as they closed in Crossman took a razor from his pocket and slit his own throat. He died on the spot.

When the trunk was opened, it was found to contain the remains of Ellen Sampson, encased in cement. Crossman had bigamously married her more than a year previously – she was in fact the fifth of seven women who became his wife. It emerged that since he had married Mrs Sampson in January 1903, killing her shortly afterwards, he had also married another two ladies, one of whom had lived with Crossman in Ladysmith Avenue, little knowing that the remains of her immediate predecessor were just a few feet away decomposing in the cupboard under the stairs.

THE CAMDEN TOWN MURDER, 1907

Railway chef Bertram Shaw's job took him to Sheffield each evening and he returned to London the following morning. On the morning of 12 September 1907 he came home from work as usual to his lodgings at 29 St Paul's Road (now Agar Grove), Camden Town. There he discovered that his sitting-room had been ransacked, and when he forced open the locked door to the bedroom he found the naked body of his common-law wife, 23-year-old Phyllis Dimmock, with her throat savagely cut. History remembers this particular case as the Camden Town Murder.

Phyllis's own job fitted in nicely with Bert's. While he was working away from home, she spent the nights as a prostitute and was well known throughout the area. The Rising Sun at 120 Euston Road was known to be one of her regular haunts. For three consecutive nights before her death she had taken a ship's cook home with her, but gave an excuse for not allowing him to come home with her on the fourth. She showed him a letter which was signed Bert. It asked her to meet him that night at 8.30 p.m. in The Eagle at Camden Town. This letter was found later, as was a postcard written in the same hand. The postcard read:

Phillis Darling.
If it pleases you to meet me at 8.15p.m. at the [instead of the name Rising Sun there was a sketch of a red-nosed sun winking over the horizon]
Yours to a cinder
Alice

The partly burned letter was found in Phyllis's fireplace and the postcard turned up two days later when Bertram Shaw decided to change rooms. The Bert mentioned in the letter was not Bertram Shaw, but Phyllis had been seen in The Eagle with a young man on a regular basis during the previous weeks. He later turned out to be both Bert and Alice. The postcard was published in the newspapers and a prostitute named Ruby Young came forward to identify the work of a young artist named Robert William Thomas George Cavers Wood. Wood was confirmed by several witnesses as the young man seen in The Eagle with Phyllis on the night she died, and he had also been seen leaving 29 St Paul's Road at dawn.

Robert Wood was a talented artist. He worked as an engraver at a glassmaker's in Grays Inn Road, and also earned money as a freelance cartoonist. He lived in a comfortable home in St Pancras with his father. The trial began at the Old Bailey on 12 December before Mr Justice Grantham and Wood was defended by the brilliant Edward Marshall Hall. The circumstantial evidence against him would have been more than sufficient to convict a less likeable young man, as would the one bloodstain on his clothing, but he made a surprisingly good impression in the witness box and spent most of his time during his six-day trial sketching the proceedings.

This case was notable for the fact that this was the first occasion on which a person on trial for murder was allowed to go into the witness box and give evidence on their own behalf. Wood completely charmed the jury, stuck to his original story concerning his version of events as told to the police and they acquitted him. Nobody else was ever implicated in this murder.

OUTRAGE IN TOTTENHAM, 1909

Saturday 23 January 1909 witnessed one of the most extraordinary chases ever to take place on the streets of North London. The murder associated with it became known as the 'Tottenham Outrage' and the chase came about after a pair of Russian anarchists snatched the wages (£80, the equivalent of about £4,000 today) as they were delivered to Schnurmann's rubber factory in Chesnut Road. Having grabbed the money, Paul Hefeld and Jacob Lapidus ran down Chesnut Road with a policeman chasing after them. They turned into Scales Road, then left into Dawlish Road and right into Mitchley Road. It was there beside the Mission Hall that Hefeld shot PC Tyler; 10-year-old Ralph Jocelyn was also shot and killed as he ran for cover. Both victims were later buried in Abney Park Cemetery, Stoke Newington.

The chase continued along Park View Road, then over the railway into the marshes. The two men ran northwards until they reached Lockwood Reservoir, then, realising police reinforcements were waiting for them, they went east across Walthamstow Avenue to Chingford Road. There they hijacked a tram travelling south, still firing guns at their pursuers. The two men forced the conductor to show them how to operate the tram – the driver had fled, along with most of the passengers. The police requisitioned a milk cart in an attempt to follow the tram, but the anarchists shot the pony. They continued to fire their guns and in all over 400 rounds were discharged. Fortunately, although seventeen civilians and seven policemen were injured, no one else was killed.

The two men then made their way through the railway arch that runs across the Ching Brook, where they found themselves confronted by a 6ft fence that formed the boundary of a

Oak Cottage, Chingford, where Russian anarchist Jacob Lapidus fled during the 'Tottenham Outrage' of 1909. He shot himself in the upstairs bedroom as the police closed in on him. *(Bruce Castle Museum/Haringey Libraries, Archives and Museum Service)*

newly built housing estate. Realising they were cornered, Hefeld panicked and shot himself in the head (he died of his injuries on 18 February), but Lapidus escaped over the fence, crossed the railway lines and made his way from Beech Hall Road towards fields bordering Prestons Avenue. A public house called the Royal Oak stood at the top of the avenue. He crossed Hale End Road to the rear of the pub and followed a hedge bordering some cottages. He leaped over this hedge and entered Oak Cottage, the home of coal carrier Charles Rolstone and his family. He ran upstairs and locked himself in the front bedroom. Several shots were exchanged but as the police closed in on him, Lapidus shot himself dead.

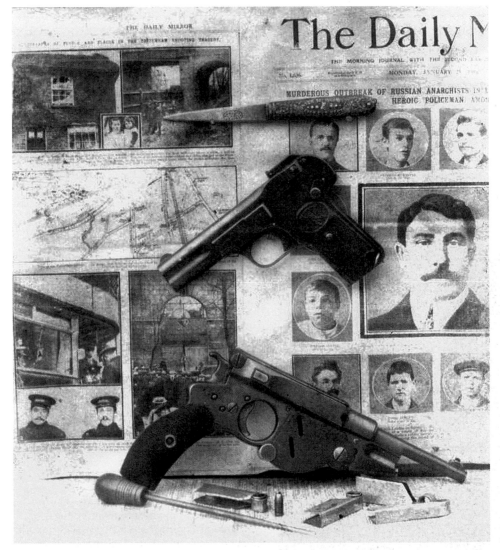

Weapons used by the Russian anarchists during the 'Tottenham Outrage'. *(Bruce Castle Museum/Haringey Libraries, Archives and Museum Service)*

ENTOMBED IN THE BATH, REGENT'S PARK, 1922

In the late summer of 1922 Mrs Alice Middleton lodged with Cecil Maltby, a tailor, who lived above his shop at 24 Park Road, which runs from Lord's cricket ground to the top of Baker Street. Although Maltby had inherited his father's business, he had allowed it to decline to the point of bankruptcy. His wife and children had left him and he found solace in heavy drinking. Not long after Mrs Middleton came to live with him, he shot her (probably to obtain her ready cash) and put her body in the bath. He then covered the bath over and used it as a dining table. Neighbours complained about the declining state of the premises and the increasingly insanitary conditions. When a sanitary inspector obtained a warrant the police broke in, at which point Maltby shot himself. The entire place was in a filthy state and Mrs Maltby's putrefying remains were discovered in the bath beneath the 'dining table'.

KILLED BY HER ONE-LEGGED LOVER, CAMDEN TOWN, 1926

On New Year's Day 1926 in a house in Arlington Road, Camden Town, 17-year-old Polly Edith Walker was discovered by her widowed mother lying beneath her bed in her nightdress. She had been strangled with one of her own silk stockings by her 25-year-old, French-Canadian, one-legged street musician lover Eugene de Vere, also known as Ewen Stitchell. Polly had also sustained severe head injuries. A copper-handled poker was found lying on the blood-soaked eiderdown, as were some broken fire tongs.

De Vere was almost a vagrant and Polly, who felt sorry for him, had taken him under her wing. Following his arrest at Hitchin in Hertfordshire on Sunday 3 January, he admitted killing her out of jealousy following the discovery that she had taken another lover. *The Times* reported that, despite his artificial left leg, de Vere is believed to have walked the 32 miles to Hitchin after murdering Polly. He was hanged at Pentonville on 24 March 1926.

BURNED BODY FOUND IN A SHED, CAMDEN TOWN, 1933

On the evening of Tuesday 3 January 1933 a garden shed at 30 Hawley Crescent, Camden Town, was the scene of an appalling murder, which the perpetrator had attempted to disguise as his own suicide. Inside the partially burned shed, sitting at a desk, were the charred remains of a man's body. The shed, which was divided into two portions, had been rented as an office by unsuccessful businessman, builder and decorator Samuel Furnace.

A suicide note meant to create the impression that the body was that of Mr Furnace read: 'Goodbye all. No work. No money. Sam J. Furnace.' However, suspicion was aroused when a bullet wound was discovered in the corpse's back and the teeth of the deceased were of a man considerably younger than Furnace's 42 years. A post-mortem examination revealed that the dead man had been shot twice. Further investigation showed him to be a 25-year-old rent collector, Walter Spatchett, who lived with his parents in Dartmouth Park Road, Highgate.

A nationwide hunt was instigated for Furnace on 9 January. He was eventually caught in Southend and brought back to Kentish Town police station. He claimed that the killing had been accidental. Locked in a cell overnight he asked if he could have his overcoat, as it was particularly cold. When the coat was brought to him he took out a phial of hydrochloric acid which he had secreted in the lining and drank the contents. He was taken to hospital where doses of morphine were administered to ease his suffering, but he never regained consciousness and died about 24 hours later on Tuesday 17 January in St Pancras Hospital.

His body was taken to St Pancras Mortuary where an autopsy was carried out by Sir Bernard Spilsbury. A coroner's jury later concluded that Spatchett's death was not accidental and that Furnace was guilty of his murder.

THE BODY IN THE WAREHOUSE CELLAR, ISLINGTON, 1937

In 1937 Frederick Murphy lived at 57a Colebrooke Row and worked for Harding's, a furnishing company at 22 The Green, Islington. On 14 May he reported to his employers that he had discovered a dead woman in the cellar of their warehouse. When the police arrived, Murphy had left the scene.

The body was identified as prostitute Rosina Field. She habitually took a room at 13 Duncan Terrace and had last done so on 11 May. Frederick Murphy turned up at Poplar police station the next day. He had bloodstains on his clothes and told the police that he had been on a pub crawl at the time Field was killed. However, witnesses came forward to say that they had seen Murphy entering the warehouse with Rosina Field at the time he claimed to have been drinking elsewhere.

This was not the only time that Murphy had found himself linked to a murdered prostitute. He had been accused of murder before when he had been seen in the company of Katherine Peck, known as 'Carbolic Kate', shortly before she had been found in Aldgate with her throat cut. Murphy was fortunate on that occasion, as the main witness for the prosecution disappeared. However, he was not so lucky this time. He was found guilty of the murder of Rosina Field and hanged at Pentonville on 17 August 1937.

SAVED FROM THE GALLOWS, SOUTHGATE, 1948

In the early evening of St Valentine's Day, 14 February 1948, in Wade's Hill, Southgate, 33-year-old PC Nathaniel Edgar was on plain-clothes patrol duty following a spate of burglaries in the area. Shots were heard and passers-by reported the sound of running footsteps along Broadlands Avenue. PC Edgar was found dying outside 112 Wade's Hill.

Before he died he managed to whisper the name of his murderer, which he had also managed to write in his notebook along with his identity number. He was 23-year-old army deserter Donald George Edgar. The man was traced to a boarding house in Stockwell through the publication of a photograph of a married woman, Mrs Winkless, with whom he was having an affair. When he was arrested he was in bed; a gun was found under his pillow. He was tried and convicted of murder, but was uniquely reprieved because Parliament was testing abolition of the death penalty and the trial took place during the five-year suspension period.

ESCAPE FROM THE GALLOWS ON GROUNDS OF REASONABLE DOUBT, FINCHLEY, 1949

In 1949 Brian Donald Hume, a second-hand-car dealer, murdered his business associate Stanley Setty by stabbing him with a Nazi SS dagger at 620b Finchley Road. He cut up the body and put it into three parcels which he weighted with bricks. He then flew the parcels over the English Channel and dropped them into the sea.

One parcel washed up at Burnham-on-Crouch, Essex, and fingerprints from the hands in the package identified the victim as Setty, who had already been reported missing. At his trial Hume claimed to know nothing about the murder, but said he had agreed to dispose of the parcels for three crooks he named as Greeny, Mac and 'The Boy'. The jury acquitted him on grounds of reasonable doubt. He was, however, sentenced as an accessory to the crime and jailed for twelve years. He served eight of them, receiving the maximum remission for good behaviour. He was released from Dartmoor in the spring of 1958.

Once he was out of gaol he admitted that he had invented the crooks and had simply based his descriptions of them on the detectives who had interviewed him. His confession was printed in four issues of the *Sunday Pictorial*, which was reputed to have paid him £2,000 for the story. Under English law he could not be tried again for the same crime, and with the proceeds made from his confession he went to live in Switzerland. He returned to the United Kingdom to commit two armed robberies, one on 2 August 1959 when he held up the Midland Bank at Brentford in Middlesex, getting away with over £1,000, and the second at another Midland Bank on the Great West Road. This time he escaped with very little money, having shot and seriously wounded the manager.

He returned to Switzerland, where he murdered again, shooting a taxi driver during a bank robbery in 1959. There was no death penalty there. Instead he was sentenced to life imprisonment with hard labour. In August 1976 the Swiss authorities judged him insane and returned him to Britain, where he was incarcerated in Broadmoor. In 1988, at the age of 67 and considered low risk, he was moved to a hospital in West London.

STYLLOU CHRISTOFI: MURDER IN HAMPSTEAD, 1954

By coincidence the last two women to be hanged in Britain committed murder in the same street in Hampstead just nine months apart. The first was carried out by Mrs Styllou Christofi, who killed her 36-year-old daughter-in-law in July 1954; the second, committed in April 1955, was the tragic case of Ruth Ellis, who shot her lover David Blakely (see Chapter 8).

In 1954 the ground floor and first floor of 11 South Hill Park, Hampstead, were occupied by the family of a Greek Cypriot named Stavros Christofi, who worked as a wine waiter at the famous Café de Paris in London's West End. Stavros lived there with his German wife Hella and their three children. The Christofis had been married for about fifteen years when, in 1953, his mother came over from Cyprus to live with them. Her intention was to make enough money to pay off a mortgage on a property she owned, and to that end she managed to get a job at a ladies' belt manufacturers at 3 Helena Road, Willesden. Styllou Pantopiou Christofi was illiterate even in her own language; unable or unwilling to learn English or German, she had great difficulty communicating with her daughter-in-law and relied on conveying what she needed to through her son, to whom she clung jealously. Hella became the object of Mrs Christofi's obsessive jealousy and hatred.

There is no doubt that Mrs Christofi was a horrible woman to have as a mother-in-law – and she knew all about mothers-in-law: in 1925, while two fellow villagers had held open the mouth of her own mother-in-law, Mrs Christofi had rammed a blazing torch down her throat, killing her. (She was, apparently, acquitted of the crime.) Stavros had already found it necessary to lodge his mother elsewhere, but on the two occasions he had found her alternative accommodation she had proved so objectionable that she had been returned to them in South Hill Park. The situation became intolerable between the two women and it was decided that when Hella took the children on holiday to Germany later that summer, Stavros would arrange for his mother to return to Cyprus for good.

On the evening of 29 July 1954, while Stavros was at work and the children were in bed, Mrs Christofi murdered Hella by hitting her on the head with a cast-iron ash plate. She then set about burning the body in the garden. When the remains were examined it was discovered that Hella's skull had been fractured and there were marks of strangulation on her throat. John Young, a neighbour who lived at No. 15, had smelled paraffin and seen Mrs Christofi poking what appeared to be a tailor's dummy. Some time later Mrs Christofi stopped a passing motorist and in broken English told a pathetic tale. She said: 'Please come, fire burning, children sleeping.' When the police came, the blood and other evidence in the kitchen told an entirely different story.

Mrs Christofi was tried at the central Criminal Court before Mr Justice Devlin. She refused to plead insanity and was found to be sane by the three doctors who examined her. On 28 October the jury, having considered their verdict for a little over two hours, found her guilty of murder. She was executed at Holloway Prison on 15 December 1954 by Albert Pierrepoint.

DEATH OUTSIDE THE DANCING ACADEMY, HOLLOWAY, 1958

On 14 December 1958, in the early days of the 'Teddy Boy' era, trouble flared up between two rival gangs, the Angel Mob and the Finsbury Park Lot, outside Eugene Grey's Dancing Academy at 133 Seven Sisters Road, near that part of Holloway known as Nag's Head. Matters got out of hand and the police intervened.

Ronald Marwood, a 25-year-old scaffolder who lived in Huntingdon Street, Islington, with his 20-year-old wife Rosalie, got carried away in the events that followed. While 6ft 5in, 23-year-old PC Raymond Summers was arresting his best friend, Marwood pulled a knife out and stabbed the officer in the back. Summers died.

The boys all fled the scene, and Marwood managed to evade the law by hiding out with some friends in Chalk Farm, but the killing of a policeman was a very serious matter indeed, and Marwood's absence from home threw suspicion his way. He gave himself up after the police issued a picture of him on 3 January 1959 and he was charged with murder. He was convicted of the capital murder of a policeman, and at the Old Bailey on 19 March Ronald Marwood became the first person to be sentenced to death under the section of the Homicide Act of 1957 that protected police officers and warders. The *London Evening Standard* reported on Wednesday 6 May 1959:

> There will be no reprieve for Ronald Henry Marwood, the 25-year-old Islington Scaffolder, who knifed to death P-c Raymond Summers in a gang fight outside a Holloway dance hall. Marwood will be hanged on Friday. Mr Butler, the Home Secretary, announced his decision today in a letter to Mr Albert Evans, Socialist MP for South West Islington. Mr Evans presented to the Home Secretary a reprieve petition signed by 150 MPs – six Tories, one Liberal and 143 Socialists.

Marwood was hanged at Pentonville on Friday 8 May 1959. That day the *Evening News* reported:

> Seven hundred people crowded outside Pentonville Prison to-day when Ronald Marwood was hanged for the murder of Raymond Summers, a Holloway policeman. Mounted police had to ride into part of the crowd which began to fight with police on foot. Blows and kicks were exchanged as reinforcements arrived.

Bibliography and Sources

1.   Death of a Magistrate: The Killing of Sir Edmund Berry Godfrey

Coward, Barry, *The Stuart Age* (Longman, London, 1980)
Hill, C.P., *Who's Who in Stuart Britain* (Shepheard-Walwyn, London, 1988)
Kenyon, J.P., *The Stuarts* (B.T. Batsford, London, 1958)
Marshall, Alan, *The Strange Death of Edmund Godfrey* (Sutton Publishing, Stroud, 1999)

2.   Murder of Innocents

Downie, R. Angus, *Murder in London – A Topographical Guide to Famous Crimes* (Arthur
    Barker, London, 1973)
Pinks, William John, *The History of Clerkenwell* (2nd edition, n.p., 1880)
Sugden, Keith (ed.), *Criminal Islington* (Islington Archaeology & History Society, London, 1989)
Islington Daily Gazette and North London Tribune, Friday 2 and Monday 19 January 1903

3.   Britain's First Railway Murder: Franz Müller and the Murder of
Thomas Briggs

Bland, James, *The Common Hangman* (Ian Henry Publications, Hornchurch, 1984)
Griffiths, Arthur, *The Chronicles of Newgate* (Chapman and Hall, London, 1883)
Irving, H.B. (ed.), *Notable English Trials: Franz Müller* (William Hodge & Company,
    London, 1911)
Daily Telegraph, Monday 5 September 1864
Times, The, 11 July, 11 and 15 November 1864

4.   Undone by a Toy Lantern: Milsom and Fowler and the Murder of
Henry Smith

Garland, John, *Crimes that Thrilled the World* (Mellifont Press, London, 1937)
Honeycombe, Gordon, *The Murders of the Black Museum, 1870–1970* (Bloomsbury,
    London, 1982)
Piper, Leonard, *Murder by Gaslight* (Michael O'Mara, London, 1991)
Evening News, London, 14, 15, 17, 19–22 and 24 February, 7 and 26 March, 7, 9, 13, 14,
    16, 23, 29 and 30 April, 1, 4, 6, 7, 16, 19–22, 26 and 29 May, 5 and 9 June 1896
Evening Standard, London, 14, 15 and 17 February, 13, 14 and 17 April, 19–21 May,
    9 June 1896
Penny Illustrated Paper and Illustrated Times, The, 18 April 1896
Times, The, 15 February, 20–22 May, 10–11 June, 1896

5.   The First Murderer Caught by Wireless: The Case of Dr Crippen

Files relating to the Crippen case opened to the public in 1986 can be consulted at the
National Archives, Kew: Old Bailey Records CRIM1/117, Scotland Yard Files MEPO3/198,
Director of Public Prosecutions DPP1/13

Dew, Walter, *I Caught Crippen* (Blackie & Son, London & Glasgow, 1938)
Engel, Howard, *Lord High Executioner* (Firefly Books, Willowdale, Ontario, 1996)
Goodman, Jonathan (compiler), *The Crippen File* (Allison & Busby, London, 1985)
Honeycombe, Gordon, *The Murders of the Black Museum, 1870–1970* (Bloomsbury,
    London, 1982)

Le Neve, Ethel, *Ethel Le Neve: Her Life Story with the True Account of their Flight and her Friendship with Dr. Crippen*, first published in *Lloyd's Weekly News* of 6 and 13 November, 1910, and by John Long Ltd, London, 1910. (This edition published by the Daisy Bank Printing & Publishing Co. Gorton, Manchester, 1911.)

Sugden, Keith (ed.), *Criminal Islington* (Islington Archaeology & History Society, London, 1989)

Wallace, Edgar, William Le Queux, Herbert Vivian, Sir Max Pemberton, Trevor Allen, Sir John Hall and Edgar Jepson, *Famous Crimes of Recent Times* (George Newnes Limited, London, n.d.)

Wilson, Colin and Damon, *World Famous Crimes of Passion* (Robinson, London, 1992)

Young, Filson (ed.), *Notable British Trials: The Trial of Hawley Harvey Crippen* (William Hodge & Company, London, Edinburgh and Glasgow, 1920)

Daily Mail 16, 18, 19 and 25–30 July, 1–3 and 6 August 1910

Evening News, London, 18–22 and 25 October, 23 November 1910; 14 December 1974

Islington Gazette, 14 May 1963

Morning Advertiser, 15 July 1910

Times, The, 25 and 29 July, 2 August, 19–22, 24 and 26 October, 21, 23 and 24 November 1910

The Last Secret of Dr Crippen (Justabout Productions, 2002), shown on Channel 4, Saturday 17 July 2004

6.   Murder by Arsenical Poisoning? The Killing of Eliza Barrow

Honeycombe, Gordon, *The Murders of the Black Museum, 1870–1970* (Bloomsbury, London, 1982)

Piper, Leonard, *Murder by Gaslight* (Michael O'Mara, London, 1991)

Sugden, Keith (ed.), *Criminal Islington* (Islington Archaeology & History Society, London, 1989)

Young, Filson (ed.), *Notable British Trials: The Seddons* (William Hodge & Company, London, Edinburgh and Glasgow, 1914)

Evening News, London, 4–9 and 12–15 March, 18 April 1912

Evening Standard and St James's Gazette, 4–9 and 11–14 March, 18 April 1912

Times, The, 5, 6, 8, 9 and 11–15 March 1912

7.   The Brides in the Bath Murderer: George Joseph Smith

Honeycombe, Gordon, *The Murders of the Black Museum, 1870–1970* (Bloomsbury, London, 1982)

Sugden, Keith (ed.), *Criminal Islington* (Islington Archaeology & History Society, London, 1989)

Various authors, *Infamous Murders* (first published in Britain in 1975 by Verdict Press)

Watson, Eric R. (ed.), *Notable British Trials: George Joseph Smith* (William Hodge & Company, London, Edinburgh and Glasgow, 1915)

Daily Mirror, 24 March and 2 July 1915

News of the World, 27 December 1914; 7 February and 27 June 1915

Times, The, 13 December 1899

'The Brides in the Bath', *Real-Life Crimes and How They Were Solved*, Issue 12 (Eaglemoss Publications, London, 2003)

Murder in the UK, www.murderuk.com

8.   The Tragic Story of Ruth Ellis and the Killing of David Blakely

Ellis, Georgie, *Ruth Ellis, My Mother* (Smith Gryphon, London, 1995)

Fido, Martin, *Deadly Jealousy* (Headline, London, 1993)
Goodman, Jonathan and Patrick Pringle, *The Trial of Ruth Ellis* (Chivers Press, Bath, 1974)
Hancock, Robert, *Ruth Ellis* (Weidenfeld & Nicolson, London, 1963)
Lane, Brian, *The Murder Guide* (Robinson, London, 1991)
Marks, Laurence and Tony Van den Bergh, *Ruth Ellis* (McDonald & James, London, 1977)
Pierrepoint, Albert, *Executioner Pierrepoint* (George G. Harrap, London, 1974)
Wilson, Colin and Damon, *World Famous Crimes of Passion* (Robinson, London, 1992)
Daily Mirror, 13 and 14 July 1955
Times, The, 14 July 1955
www.crimelibrary.com/classics2/ellis

9. Death of a Playwright: Kenneth Halliwell and the Murder of Joe Orton

Lahr, John, *Prick Up Your Ears* (Penguin, London, 1978)
—— (ed.), *The Orton Diaries* (Methuen, London, 1986)
Lane, Brian, *The Murder Guide* (Robinson, London, 1991)
Daily Mail, 10 August 1967
Daily Telegraph, 10 and 19 August 1967
Evening Standard, 4 September 1967
North London Press, 18 May 1962
Times, The, 10 August 1967

10. A Miscellany

Bland, James, *The Common Hangman* (Ian Henry, Hornchurch, 1984)
Downie, R. Angus, *Murder in London – A Topographical Guide to Famous Crimes* (Arthur Barker, London, 1973)
Garland, John, *Crimes that Thrilled the World* (Mellifont Press, London, 1937)
Harris, J.D., *Outrage! An Edwardian Tragedy* (Wilson Harris, London, 2000)
Honeycombe, Gordon, *The Murders of the Black Museum, 1870–1970* (Bloomsbury, London, 1982)
Sugden, Keith (ed.), *Criminal Islington* (Islington Archaeology & History Society, London, 1989)
Daily Mirror, 30 January 1909
Evening News, London, 15–19 December 1958; 1 and 8 May 1959
Evening Standard, London, 26 January 1950; 15 and 18 December 1958; 1, 6 and 8 May 1959
Times, The, 25 October, 13, 14 and 24 December 1890; 2, 14–16, 18–19 December 1899; 10 January 1900; 14, 16–19 December 1907; 25 and 26 January 1909; 5 and 9 January 1926; 4, 5, 9, 11, 18 January 1933; 16 February 1948; 30 and 31 July, 27 and 29 October, 14 and 16 December 1954; 6 and 9 May 1959
'Mother-in-Law From Hell', *Real Life Crimes and How They Were Solved*, Issue 48 (Eaglemoss Publications, London, n.d.)
'I Got Away With Murder', *Real Life Crimes And How They Were Solved*, Issue 57 (Eaglemoss Publications, London, n.d.)

FURTHER GENERAL READING

Butler, Ivan, *Murderers' London* (Robert Hale, London, 1973)
Fido, Martin, *Murder Guide to London* (Grafton, London, 1986)
——, *The Chronicle of Crime* (Carlton, London, 1993)
Gaute, J.H.H., and Robin Odell, *The New Murderers' Who's Who* (Harrap, London, 1989)
Lane, Brian, *The Murder Guide* (Robinson, London, 1988)

Acknowledgements

For their help with this book, my thanks to: Iris Ackroyd, Keith Atack, Vera Atack, Michael Barrett, Jan Barrs, Johnny Barrs, Edward Black, Anna Blackburn, Joan Bostwick, Keith Bostwick (1931–2004), Norma Braddick, Sarah Bryce, Robert (Bob) A. Dale, Kathleen Dale, Iris Deller, Ricky S. Deller, Tracy P. Deller, Joanna C. Murray Deller, Simon Fletcher, James Friend, Andy Gaffey, Hugh Garnsworthy, Ken Gay, Jeff Gerhardt, John Goldfinch, Doris Hayes, Deborah Hedgecock, John Hinshlewood of Hornsey Historical Society, Doreen Howse, John (Jack) Howse (1922–2004), Kathleen Howse, Leah Insua, Eleanor Nelder, Stanley Nelder, Dr Declan O'Reilly, Reshma, Jenny Ridge, Michelle Tilling, Brian Gregory Thomas (1943–2004), Naomi Tummons, Hilary Walford, Adam R. Walker, Christine Walker, Darren J. Walker, David Walker, Ivan P. Walker, Paula L. Walker, Suki B. Walker, Julie Wiggett, Clifford Willoughby, Margaret Willoughby, Roy Young. Thanks also to the Trustees of the Joe Orton Estate, the staff at Bruce Castle Museum (Haringey Libraries, Archives and Museum Services), Hornsey Historical Society, the staff of Islington Local History Centre at Finsbury Library, the staff of the British Library and the staff of the National Archives, Kew.

I would also like to extend my particular thanks to John D. Murray, who has assisted me over many years.

Paul T. Langley Welch, who has taken some of the more recent photographs featured in this book, works as a freelance theatrical and commercial photographer. He has worked with me on many projects since the 1980s and has taken photographs for several of my books.